Citizens or Consumers?

What the Media Tell Us about Political Participation

I S S U E S in CULTURAL and MEDIA STUDIES

Series editor: Stuart Allan

Published titles

News Culture, 2nd edition
Stuart Allan

Modernity and Postmodern Culture
Jim McGuigan

Television, Globalization and Cultural Identities
Chris Barker

Ethnic Minorities and the Media
Edited by Simon Cottle

Cinema and Cultural Modernity
Gill Branston

Compassion, Morality and the Media
Keith Tester

Masculinities and Culture
John Beynon

Cultures of Popular Music
Andy Bennett

Media, Risk and Science
Stuart Allan

Violence and the Media
Cynthia Carter and C. Kay Weaver

Moral Panics and the Media
Chas Critcher

Cities and Urban Cultures
Deborah Stevenson

Cultural Citizenship
Nick Stevenson

Culture on Display
Bella Dicks

Critical Readings: Media and Gender
Edited by Cynthia Carter and Linda Steiner

Critical Readings: Media and Audiences
Edited by Virginia Nightingale and Karen Ross

Media and Audiences
Karen Ross and Virginia Nightingale

Critical Readings: Sport, Culture and the Media
Edited by David Rowe

Sport, Culture and the Media, 2nd edition
David Rowe

Rethinking Cultural Policy
Jim McGuigan

Media, Politics and the Network Society
Robert Hassan

Television and Sexuality
Jane Arthurs

Identity and Culture
Chris Weedon

Media and Society: Critical Perspectives
Graeme Burton

Media Discourse
Donald Matheson

Citizens or Consumers?

What the Media Tell Us about Political Participation

Justin Lewis, Sanna Inthorn and Karin Wahl-Jorgensen

Open University Press

Open University Press
McGraw-Hill Education
McGraw-Hill House
Shoppenhangers Road
Maidenhead
Berkshire
England
SL6 2QL

email: enquiries@openup.co.uk
world wide web: www.openup.co.uk

and Two Penn Plaza, New York, NY 10121-2289, USA

First published 2005

Copyright © Justin Lewis, Sanna Inthorn and Karin Wahl-Jorgensen 2005

A catalogue record of this book is available from the British Library

ISBN-10: 0 335 21555 6 (pb)   0335 21556 4 (hb)
ISBN-13: 9780335215553 (pb)   9780335215560 (hb)

Library of Congress Cataloging-in-Publication Data
CIP data applied for

Typeset by RefineCatch Limited, Bungay, Suffolk
Printed in the UK by Bell & Bain Ltd, Glasgow

Contents

List of tables

Series Editor's Preface

Discourses of 'the public' are intricately interwoven throughout the fabric of our social world. To the extent we consider ourselves to be 'members of the public', we necessarily inhabit a form of collective identity. In so doing we are claiming to occupy – however tangentially – a civic role with certain corresponding entitlements, obligations and responsibilities. Typically this role is described using a language of citizenship, although there is no easy definition of what it should entail beyond the casting of a vote in a ballot box every now and then. And this when democracy, as we all know, is about much more than elections. Its life-blood finds expression in a number of different ways, not least in the lived relations of dialogue and debate which bind us irrevocably to one another in the shared – yet always contested – ideal of 'public opinion' at the heart of civic life.

At a time when alarm bells are being sounded about the very future of democratic values, Justin Lewis, Sanna Inthorn and Karin Wahl-Jorgensen's *Citizens or Consumers? What the Media Tell Us about Political Participation* represents a bold intervention. This book enters squarely into the current controversy about the declining number of people engaged in the conventional political process. Based on the first comprehensive study of the way citizens are represented in the news, it provides powerful evidence that while the news media may not be responsible for this decline, they are doing little to help remedy it. Although many people *do* have clear ideas about politics and matters of public policy, the authors argue, the news media are much more likely to present citizens as passive, incoherent or disengaged. Their research into news reporting suggests that the idea of the citizen has been more or less eclipsed by the figure of the *consumer*. So while we hear a great deal about the 'consumer confidence' on which economies depend, we hear very little about the 'citizen confidence' on which democracies depend. Consequently, in identifying ways forward, the authors outline practical proposals for providing more democratic news media in the interest of re-engaging citizens in the politics of the everyday.

The *Issues in Cultural and Media Studies* series aims to facilitate a diverse range of critical investigations into pressing questions considered to be central to current thinking and research. In light of the remarkable speed at which the conceptual agendas of cultural and media studies are changing, the series is committed to contributing to what is an ongoing process of re-evaluation and critique. Each of the books is intended to provide a lively, innovative and comprehensive introduction to a specific topical issue from a fresh perspective. The reader is offered a thorough grounding in the most salient debates indicative of the book's subject, as well as important insights into how new modes of enquiry may be established for future explorations. Taken as a whole, then, the series is designed to cover the core components of cultural and media studies courses in an imaginatively distinctive and engaging manner.

Stuart Allan
Series Editor

1 Democracy, citizenship and the media

Robert Putnam, in his book *Bowling Alone*, argues that we are witnessing a decline in civic participation in all aspects of community life. He sees civil society disintegrating, as the organisations and activities that define social democratic life begin to decline and wither away. The decline of Bowling Leagues in the USA thus becomes a metaphor for a society that he sees becoming less participatory and more individualistic and fragmented. To support his thesis, Putnam presents the reader with a wealth of evidence suggesting that community-based and civic activity – whether it belongs to the PTA or a political party – is being replaced by individual or domestic forms of leisure or consumption. In short, rather than engaging with our fellow citizens, we are sitting at home watching TV (Putnam, 2000).

While Putman's thesis is persuasive, it is important to acknowledge that the move away from civic or community activity is not seamless or unremitting. The growth of virtual communities on the Internet, for example, has created spaces for new forms of social interaction. None the less, it is fairly clear that the 'information age' has not brought with it a more robust form of participatory democracy. Our concern, in this book, is with one of the alarming features of the trend away from civic life: the fact that basic forms of democratic decision-making have become passé. As fewer and fewer people take part in elections, we are confronted with an image of isolated figures in polling booths, paying their last respects to the old-fashioned ritual of voting.

There is no doubt that in most countries patterns of electoral participation have followed a steady downward trend. In the United States, presidential elections, for all the expense, advertising blitz and razzmatazz, usually involve only half the electorate. The expectations for other elections – for Congress or state governance – are even lower. And while the 2004 presidential election signalled an increase in turnout, this looks much more like a temporary respite than a reversal. The 2004 election, after all, involved two candidates neck and neck in the polls for much of the campaign, an electorate sharply divided on a range of issues – including their involvement in a controversial war – and unprecedented levels of financial and human resources devoted to getting the vote out. The 2004 election was repeatedly described as a pivotal moment in deciding the country's future direction (not least by the rest of the world, in what was a massive global media event). Indeed, it is hard to imagine, in the context of the current US electoral system, more propitious conditions for encouraging participation. And yet, for all this, 40% of the US electorate still did not vote.

Indeed, a percentage that was hailed as a 'record' turnout in the USA (a record only because the US electorate was larger in 2004 than in earlier years, when proportional turnout was higher) would have been regarded as dismal elsewhere. So, for example, in 2001, Britain recorded its lowest ever turnout (since the franchise was extended to women), with just 59% of the population voting – roughly the same as in the 2004 US presidential election. In the British general election of 2005, in spite of successful government campaigns to boost postal voting (which nearly quadrupled), turnout rose only marginally to 61% – still significantly below twentieth-century levels. And lower-profile elections in Britain – whether for the European Parliament or less newsworthy levels of government – regularly involve an active minority making decisions on behalf of the majority. By comparison, turnouts in recent elections in Denmark, Finland, Germany, Holland, Italy, Norway and Sweden (between 1998 and 2003) ranged from 70% to 87% (Sussman, 2005: 162).

Worry about low and declining voter turnouts is given added urgency by surveys that suggest that young people, in particular, are disengaged with traditional forms of democracy. A MORI survey suggested that only 39% of young people in Britain who were eligible to vote in 2001 did so (MORI, 2001) – the lowest ever recorded figure. A number of politicians, dismayed by this disinterest, have voiced their concern: as former British cabinet minister Stephen Byers put it: 'There is a danger that we could be witnessing a whole generation being lost to our democratic political process' (*Sunday Times*, 24th August 2003).

The decline in turnout has been brought into sharper focus by the success of reality television shows like *Pop Idol* and *Big Brother*, where audiences cast their votes for their favourites or to eject contestants they dislike. In 2001, the two UK *Pop Idol* finalists, Gareth Gates and Will Young, received more votes between them than the Liberal Democrats, who finished a strong third in the 2001 British general election. When Craig Philips, a 28-year-old bricklayer, won *Big Brother* in 2000, it was as a result of the biggest phone vote in British history (7.5 million people). Earlier that year, participation in British elections for the European Parliament had sunk to a new low, prompting some obvious comparisons. Writing on the front page of the *Independent*, Cahal Milmo was one of many to draw attention to 'the most intimidating statistic of the year: more people have voted in the Big Brother ejections than in the European elections' (*Independent*, 16th September 2000).

If many young people *are* more interested in using their votes to take part in reality TV shows than to elect the people who decide whether they are at war or peace, who make the laws that govern them and how public money should be spent, then what is to become of democracy? How representative can a government be if whole sections of the population take no part in the process?

Before we accept this vision of democracy in decline, we should add a few caveats. First of all, voting in a reality television show and in an election are not mutually exclusive. The first does *not* signal a decadent disinterest in the second. There is, secondly, the question of how we define democracy, and what constitutes citizen engagement. There is evidence that the increasing number of people abstaining from the electoral process do so less out of a disengagement with politics than with a contempt for politicians (Henn and Weinstein, 2002). So, for example, the global demonstrations that took place against the war in Iraq in February 2003 were huge exercises in mass political expression. These involved the biggest mass protests ever seen in Britain and across the rest of Europe – hardly the sign of an apathetic public turning away from politics. And yet there is no doubt that the willingness of people to take to the streets does not seem to be matched by an enthusiasm for more conventional politics.

This may partly be because declining turnouts are a product of a political system in which the ideological differences between the main parties have narrowed. A survey of potential first-time voters in Britain by Matt Henn and Mark Weinstein found a majority felt that the 'main political parties in Britain don't offer voters real choices in elections because their policies are pretty much all the same' (*ibid.*: 6). In particular, we have seen many of the main left-leaning or socialist parties in Europe and North America shift to the right, leaving the large bloc of left-leaning voters – especially in countries with electoral systems that favour big parties – feeling disenfranchised. This is most obvious in 'first past the post' electoral systems like those in Britain and the USA, where voters are discouraged from choosing smaller parties that might better reflect their views because the winner takes all.

So, for example, neither of the main parties in the USA advocates the kind of universal, national health system adopted by most developed countries (and, in the past, by Democrats like President Truman), leaving the solid bloc of voters who favour such a system with no viable candidates to choose from (Lewis, 2001). And in Britain, the many people who tell pollsters that they are unhappy with the increasing role of private companies in public services can no longer express this view by voting Labour.

Mainstream politicians, for their part, tend to focus blame elsewhere, notably on the news media, which they see as fostering cynicism in politics. This has been especially the case in Britain, where a confrontational style and the tendency to accentuate the negative has come in for much criticism (epitomised by the BBC's Jeremy Paxman's well-known attitude toward political interviews: 'why is this lying bastard lying to me?'). Even in the USA, where the broadcast/broadsheet news media tend to treat leading politicians far more gently, the words 'politics' and 'politicians' have become pejorative terms. This has allowed celebrity candidates like Arnold Schwarzenegger to successfully flaunt their *lack of* political experience as a virtue.

But cynicism toward politicians and politics is not simply a function of journalistic disrespect. Indeed, many would argue that senior politicians are too often given an easy ride, and that the news media should be *more* rigorous than they are in calling them to account. This is most often argued in relation to the USA, where Robert McChesney's analysis of large US media corporations and government suggests that the relationship between them is cosy rather than adversarial (McChesney, 2000). So, for example, Richard Maxwell, writing about the failure of the news media to scrutinise the many corporate beneficiaries of the 'economic stimulus package' passed in 2001, argued that:

> The corporate media's silence on this issue gives further evidence that rich media do not work for democratic ends . . . and only contribute to enlightened debate on subjects of vital interest to US citizens if their own interests are not threatened.
>
> (Maxwell, 2002: 242)

What we see here, in other words, is a lack rather than an excess of journalistic interrogation.

Even in the British context, however, the perceived tenacity of certain journalists in going after politicians is not the main source of popular cynicism. What is more corrosive, we would suggest, is the way in which *politics itself* is often framed by news media. Conflict and debate about ideas – ideological differences and divisions – is at the very heart of democratic politics. And yet conflict and division is generally cast as negative while unity and consensus is seen as positive. Genuine political divisions are all too often transformed into a stereotype of squabbling politicians more interested in 'party politics' than the common good. And political divisions *within* political parties are nearly always portrayed as problematic rather than healthy.

In this sense, when journalists complain about a culture of political 'spin' in which the modern politician is required to be tediously 'on message', they are bemoaning a culture partly of their own making. So, for example, when discussing the development of new policies on airport security in the USA, conflicting political interests and approaches to the issue were seen as a problem that needed to be overcome to achieve progress. As CBS News put it, 'Apparently feeling the heat at last, congressional negotiators finally broke a partisan deadlock today and agreed on a common approach . . .' (CBS News, 15th November 2001). Political debate, in this framework, is translated as 'partisan deadlock'. This reduces the motives and ideological differences that such debates express to the status of petty, professional divisions.

While the negative focus on conflict may make sense in terms of news values, we need to be aware that the logical outcome of such a view is to replace democratic politics with a kind of managerial meritocracy, in which we lose sight of the fact that democracy is about competing ideas and interests, and vote simply for who is the 'best' man or woman for the job. Hence studies have repeatedly shown that the coverage of politics is invariably about style, process and personality rather than the policy decisions that will actually affect people (Jackson, 1996; Deacon, Golding and Billig, 2001; Sussman, 2005). This is an oddity, if we think about it, since if politics *was* simply a question of meritocracy and management, we would be better off with a panel of experts than a popular vote. More importantly, this version of democratic politics takes the passion out of politics, and does little to inspire political interest or to make connections between politics and citizens.

In short, we would argue that leading political parties and the news media have helped to impoverish popular ideas about politics. The narrowing of ideological divisions between parties has more to do with the power of corporate pressure on politicians than with public opinion, and has left cynicism and disengagement in its wake. At the same time, the news media have, for some time, attached negative value to the conflicts that are at the very heart of political debate.

We shall return to some of these issues in later chapters. Our main purpose, in this book, however, is not to weigh up the relative merits of these explanations, but to examine a broader issue. Since most of us learn much of what we know about politics and politicians from the news media (Hargreaves and Thomas, 2002), what do the news media tell us about *our* role, as citizens, in a democracy? Are we encouraged to be active, informed citizens, contributing to public discussion and debate? Or is politics presented as something that is irrelevant to our daily lives? And if we do have opinions, is it suggested that we can influence the political process, or are we portrayed as powerless?

The media and democracy

A declining interest in representative politics has been seen as part of a more general fall in civic participation and a decreasing interest in political life (cf. Blumler and Gurevitch, 1995; Capella and Jamieson, 1997; Buckingham, 2000). In keeping with Robert Putnam's thesis, a number of scholars have linked the turn away from conventional democracy to an absence of places and opportunities for citizens to discuss politics (cf. Gamson, 1992; Eliasoph, 1998; Wahl-Jorgensen, 2002a). Thus we have seen the concept of the citizen replaced by the more limited idea of the consumer. Citizens are actively engaged in the shaping of society and the making of history; consumers simply choose between the products on display.

The terms of neo-liberal economics – with its emphasis on the corporate management of a consumer society – have thereby seeped into the public sphere. Indeed, the public domain – whether it is the places we get our news, where we shop or where we gather together – is increasingly dominated by large private corporations. Audiences and publics have become markets (even a public service broadcaster like the BBC talks the language of market shares), and while audiences can express opinions, markets can only buy – or not buy – what is on offer. As George Gerbner puts it, the stories that define our identities, communities and nations 'no longer come from families, schools, churches, neighbourhoods and often not even from the native countries, or, in fact, from anyone with anything to tell. Increasingly they come from distant conglomerates with something to sell' (Gerbner, 2002: 486).

There is, of course, a danger here of idealising a mythic past – just as Jürgen Habermas idealised a nineteenth-century public sphere in which citizens debated the issues of the day in salons and coffee houses (Habermas, 1989). People have been excluded in various ways from democratic processes – whether by custom or decree – ever since their beginnings in ancient Greece (Peters, 1995; Lewis, 2001). It would be difficult to define any period as a golden age of democracy and citizenship.

On the contrary, it could be argued that we have never lived at a time when democratic principles have been held in higher regard. It is no longer acceptable to suggest, as the British politician Thomas Macaulay did in the 1830s, that it is only the 'higher and middling orders (who) are the natural representatives of the human race' (Thompson, 1968: 905). Indeed, the widespread concern about declining turnouts and political disengagement comes from a commonly held view that broad participation is pivotal to democracy, and that both are desirable.

It is perhaps most accurate to say that although we live at a time of unprecedented democratic *possibility*, many of the trends that define contemporary life have worked *against* the development of a healthier democratic society. The corporate privatisation of media and public space, the growth of home-based entertainment and the decline of civic culture have all made the idea of citizenship less relevant to most people in their everyday lives.

At the same time we have seen the increasing commercialisation of broadcast news, where declining budgets for domestic and international news have combined with a quest for ratings in a competitive environment. This has led to widespread accusations of 'dumbing down' in the coverage of news and public affairs (e.g. Riddell, 1999; Hodgson, 2002). There is certainly evidence to support such a claim, although only in relation to commercial media. In their study of broadcast news in Britain, Ian Hargreaves and James Thomas show that while the commercial news channels take many of their stories from the tabloid press, those news broadcasters with a clear public service broadcasting remit – notably the BBC and Channel 4 – maintain a focus on international issues, politics and social policy issues (Hargreaves and Thomas, 2002: 89).

We should also be wary of adopting the phrase 'dumbing down'. The term carries with it the suggestion that there is something virtuous about reporting news that is, for many people, esoteric or difficult to understand. Worse still, it implies that making news popular or accessible is to render it banal. Clearly there *is* a case for saying that an emphasis on crime stories and celebrity culture at the expense of significant social, political or economic developments does little to encourage active citizenship. But we also need to question the value of many 'hard' news stories to people's everyday lives, as well as a style of reporting that often speaks only to an 'informed' audience, and which does little to engage people with public affairs. The Hargreaves and Thomas study, for example, found more people – particularly black and working-class respondents – agreeing than disagreeing with the statement that 'much of the news is not relevant to me' (*ibid.*: 80). This issue is central to our theme, and we shall return to it in our conclusion.

More optimistic scholars have suggested that news and political journalism continues to fulfil its democratic role (e.g. Brants, 1998; Blumler, 1999; McNair, 2000a) even if the forms it takes are both more varied and more market-oriented. So, for example, Pippa Norris (2000) has argued that political journalism generates a 'virtuous circle' of citizen participation. Her research indicates that engaged individuals consume political news, and that this consumption encourages them to become even more politically active and informed as citizens. This conclusion is borne out by other research indicating that news can play a role in informing understanding of public affairs (Neuman, Just and Crigler, 1992; Delli Carpini and Keeter, 1996; Nie, Junn, and Stehlik-Barry, 1996).

What this work *also* suggests, however, is that the people who get the most from news – who understand and absorb it – are those who already follow and understand it. Those inside the 'virtuous circle' may be becoming better equipped citizens, but they are not a representative group. They tend to be relatively privileged in social class terms, and thereby feel a closer identification to those in power. News is, in this sense, like a soap opera for the chattering classes. For those outside this circle – the more intermittent and less avid audience – news only serves to increase a sense of distance and insignificance.

This point is well made by Michael Delli Carpini and Scott Keeter in their comprehensive study *What Americans Know About Politics and Why It Matters* (1996). Their argument represents the flipside of Pippa Norris's virtuous circle, in which those who feel distant from the world of the news often end up being misinformed by it, and are consequently less able to act – or vote – in their own interests. So, for example, they describe how sections of the US population voted for candidates who they *thought* were committed to increasing spending on public services, even while the candidate's platform was actually to *decrease* such spending.

In this context, research done by Russell Neuman, Marion Just and Ann Crigler demonstrates both the positive and negative role that news can play in promoting or discouraging citizenship. On the one hand, they argue, 'part of the public's limited interest in the official side of national and international affairs results from a profound sense of powerlessness', and yet, despite this, the people in their study 'reacted with special enthusiasm to information about how to take control of public issues' (1992: 111). Similarly, work by Greg Philo suggests that while most people tend to find international news dull, their interest significantly increases when those stories are placed in a wider, more relevant, context (Philo, 2002). In short, there is nothing inevitable about the relations between the news media and people's ability or inclination to act as engaged citizens.

In this book, we shall explore the relationship between media and democracy by asking whether the routines and practices of journalism empower people to become engaged in public affairs, or whether they contribute to producing a passive, disengaged citizenry. What does the news media teach us about our fellow citizens? And what do they suggest about the role we should play in a democratic society? In a climate of declining political participation, does the role that citizens play in the news media encourage or discourage them to engage with politics and public life? Our focus here is thus on the way the citizen – and public opinion – is *represented* in news media.

Our analysis rests on the assumption that media representations do not merely *reflect* the world but also *construct* our understandings of it (cf. Gieber, 1964; Schlesinger, 1999). In other words, the way citizens – either as individuals or as members of the public – are portrayed on the news media helps to shape what it *means* to be a citizen in a democracy. Although these representations may be the outcome of time-honoured journalistic practices, they can, none the less, convey a profound political message.

We agree with Brian McNair that 'the public in a democracy should have opportunities not just to read about, or to watch and listen to the development of political debates as spectators, but to participate directly in them, through channels of access' (McNair, 2000b: 105). In a democratic system, the public are not merely passive viewers of news, but among its central characters, playing a visible and active part in the way stories are told. As Simon Cottle has suggested, those people whose 'voices and viewpoints structure and inform news discourses' go to 'the heart of democratic views of, and radical concerns about, the news media' (Cottle, 2000: 427).

News media and citizenship

Despite the central role of the news media in providing us with models of citizenship (so, for example, the coverage of politics often contains implications about what it means to be a 'good' citizen), there have been few systematic studies of the subject to date. Certainly, various aspects of this question, such as the news media's use of opinion polls, have been addressed by scholars such as Benjamin Page (1996), Susan Herbst (1998) and Justin Lewis (2001). But while opinion polls are, for all their limits, the most systematic way of finding out what citizens think about politics and public affairs, the public appear in the news in a number of different guises. As we shall see, the news media routinely refer to citizens or popular opinion *without* the use of polls. The research presented here is the first systematic exploration of the many different ways in which citizen engagement with public affairs is reported.

Media sociologists have long argued that journalism offers little room for the voices of citizens, and generally focuses instead on the activities of the powerful (cf. Epstein, 1973; Sigal, 1973; Gans, 1980). Studies of news values (Galtung and Ruge, 1999; Harcup & O'Neill, 2001; Manning, 2001) suggest that the 'actions of the elite are, at least usually and in short-term perspective, more consequential than the activities of others' (Galtung and Ruge, 1999: 25). In this context, ordinary people are only seen to be interesting as witnesses and bystanders, when, for example, they are victims of crimes or natural disasters.

There is no conspiracy here, no attempt to deliberately exclude ordinary people from the cast of characters that make up the news. On the contrary, many journalists are deeply concerned about levels of political disengagement, and are receptive to ideas about ways of reversing this trend. The problem is more deep-rooted. There is a hierarchy of access embedded in dominant news values, which is part of a system of practices and rationalisations that make journalism possible. These practices may be informal, but they are, none the less, deeply ingrained. It is for this reason that Golding and Elliott describe broadcast journalism as 'a highly regulated and routine process of manufacturing a cultural product on an electronic production line' (Golding and Elliott, 1999: 119).

Behind these practices lie two contradictory impulses. The first comes from the laudable ideal that journalism is there to inform. By this token, news is seen as being about matters of consequence. Unless an ordinary citizen does something unusual, atypical or egregious, they are, by this definition, not 'news'. At the same time comes the very different awareness that since ordinary citizens are the audience for news, so journalists must be aware of what matters to them. This second impulse has been shaped by the needs of commerce, so that 'what matters' becomes 'what is of interest'. These impulses have, between them, created a set of assumptions in which some of the original *raison d'être* of journalism is pushed to the sidelines.

What is of consequence often becomes simply a matter of *who* is of consequence. So, for example, the speeches or actions of politicians become newsworthy not because those speeches or actions are important or significant, but because the people who are making them are. Celebrity news takes this a step further: the words and actions of the famous may be inconsequential, but they are seen as *important* simply because they are *of interest*. What often gets lost in the criss-cross of journalistic imperatives is a principle essential to robust citizenship: the idea that what makes the news should be those things that affect everyday life – whether it is government policy, the environment, science and medicine, economic or social trends or cultural events.

At the bottom of this lies a debate about the purpose of journalism. Is it there to entertain or to inform, to sell or to tell? This conflict tends to be glossed over because news organisations have little time to ponder or reconcile journalistic philosophies and practices that may be at odds with each other. Even on the idealistic side of the ledger, there are contradictions. Impartiality and objectivity are often trotted out as the twin pillars of good journalism. And yet impartiality is based on a form of relativism, in which the truth is regarded as either elusive or contentious – requiring 'both sides' of the story to be told. The goal of such reporting is not truth but balance. Objectivity, on the other hand, suggests that there is a truthful, accurate account of the world against which claims can be measured. Balance is not only irrelevant to the notion of objectivity but may even impede it, in the sense that to be impartial about a misleading statement ('the moon is made of cream cheese') is to obscure rather than enlighten.

It could be argued, of course, that there are some conditions when objectivity is helpful, and some where impartiality applies. But these decisions are often made on the basis of customs and conventions rather than a set of guidelines – customs and conventions that are repeated rather than scrutinised or questioned. Jenny Kitzinger has described how journalistic frameworks for understanding issues become established and fixed, and it is these templates – rather than a set of principles – that dictate how a story is covered (Kitzinger, 2000).

So, for example, the media coverage of claims about a link between the MMR vaccine and autism in Britain in 2002 were informed by a framework – established during the crisis about 'mad cow' disease – in which the government and established medical expertise were regarded as unreliable. The watchword, in this coverage, was balance rather than objectivity – to give equal weight to claims and counter-claims about the alleged link, rather than to try to establish which claim was more plausible. This approach led to large sections of the public feeling confused and misinformed about the weight of medical evidence on the issue, which was *not*, despite public perception, evenly balanced, but overwhelmingly against the plausibility of the MMR/ autism link (Lewis and Speers, 2003).

Because of what Davis Merritt has characterised as 'the tyranny of space and time' (Merritt, 1995: 15), there are few opportunities for journalists to question these customs and practices. News organisations have developed reportorial shortcuts that make it possible for journalists to gather easily and quickly the information they need. Inevitably these shortcuts are often biased towards the statements, opinions and interpretations of those whose views are already privileged by society. Gaye Tuchman (1978: 21) suggests that the institutionalised and centralised beat reporting system is a 'news net' that catches the 'big fish' or the stories spawned by public relations experts, but lets the little tales of average people slip through the holes.

Journalists, for their part, are quick to point to their own dissatisfaction with these routine practices. Indeed, as Bonnie Brennen (1995) has suggested, the cultural discourse of journalists, captured in newsworkers' fiction writing, implies that although their work was 'sometimes exciting and adventurous, the majority of the time it was routine, repetitive, monotonous, dull, and boring' (Brennen, 1995: 91).

And yet there is a paradox here. If citizens end up being excluded, almost by definition, from ideas about what is newsworthy, why is the public still a constant referent for the way stories are reported? Our study seeks to uncover the ways in which the established routines of journalism *do* allow for regular citizens to appear on television news or in the press – as citizens, rather than victims or eyewitnesses.

The scope of the study

Throughout this book, we draw upon research from a range of traditions – from political science to the study of media and mass communication. Our focus, however, is on what is the largest and most comprehensive study of the news media's representation of public opinion and citizenship conducted to date. The research, funded by the British Economic and Social Research Council, is based on an analysis of television news and the press in both Britain and the USA. While the two countries share many cultural traditions, their broadcast news media have developed in very different circumstances: the USA is the apotheosis of a commercial approach to media, while British broadcasting is often regarded as a model of public service broadcasting (even if it has, in recent years, moved towards a more commercial approach). Our comparative approach thus allows us to see the extent to which news conventions are transatlantic or culturally specific.

We analysed, first of all, 5,658 television news stories in Britain and the

USA, concentrating our sample on well-established news bulletins with large audiences. In Britain this involved the two early national evening broadcasts on BBC and ITV (these being the two most popular television channels in Britain, whose news programmes have the largest audiences). In the USA, we examined the three main network news programmes: *ABC World News Tonight*, *CBS Evening News* and *NBC Nightly News* (also all broadcast during the early evening), on the three most popular US television channels.

We are aware, of course, that there are news media – notably radio and forms of new media – that are more interactive, and invoke citizenship more directly. Our choice of the most popular forms of news does not, therefore, provide an exhaustive description of the 'newsworld'. Our focus is on the most commonly consumed and influential form of news (Hargreaves and Thomas, 2002), rather than a diverse range of news sources.

The sample originally involved all the weekday UK and US television news programmes over a period of three and a half months – chosen in advance – between 30th October 2001 until mid-February 2002. Due to the attack on the World Trade Center and the Pentagon on September 11th 2001 we decided to expand our US news sample back to 12th September so that the US sample covered a five-month period.

The fact that the aftermath of the September 11th attacks and the subsequent 'war on terrorism' fell within our time frame also allowed us to pay special attention to the way citizens are represented during a period of 'national crisis' and when key decisions are being made by governments about war, peace and security (see Chapter 7). While terrorism remained a big story throughout the time period of our analysis – as it still does today – it was also a long enough period for the resumption of normal patterns of news reporting (i.e. without single or unusual events dominating the news). We were aware, in our analysis, of the way the post-September 11th period – especially in the USA – might influence the data, and so we have paid special attention to the consistency of patterns over time and in comparisons between the USA and Britain.

In our analysis of broadcast news our goal was ambitious: to analyse *every* reference to citizenship or public opinion, whether implicit or direct. This posed a serious challenge. While overt references to citizens through mechanisms like opinion polls are easy to identify, more subtle inferences about public opinion, such as 'there's a widespread feeling that . . .' or 'most people think that . . .' are difficult to find without a close reading of every item in a news programme. One of our first tasks was therefore to identify the various ways in which citizens are invoked. To do this, we began with the categories used by Brookes, Lewis and Wahl-Jorgensen in their study of how citizens were represented in the 2001 British general election (Brookes, Lewis and Wahl-Jorgensen, 2004), and developed and extended those categories to encompass our larger, more varied sample.

Once we adopted this fairly inclusive definition of citizenship and public opinion, it became clear that references to citizens in the television news media are both routine and commonplace. Within the 5,658 television news items we looked at, we found 4,398 distinct and identifiable references to citizens or public opinion. Since some stories involved several references and others none, the pattern of representation was patchy and clustered. None the less, during an average week, around 30–40% of stories in both countries made *some* reference to citizens or publics.

In terms of breakdown by country, the US television sample consisted of 2,880 references (which came from a data set of five months of coverage on three channels, or fifteen months of coverage overall), and the UK sample consisted of 1,518 references (which came from a data set of three and half months of coverage on two channels, or seven months of coverage overall). The US sample was larger because it involved three programmes rather than two, and included the period from 12th September to 29th October 2001.

The overall volume of references to citizens and publics in the USA and Britain was similar: British news programmes involved 216 references per month of weekday news programmes, and the US 192 references per month of weekday news programmes (a difference that narrows when we consider that US news programmes, while taking a similar half-hour slot, are shorter due to the frequency of commercial breaks). In what follows, we will explore any divergence between US and British TV news reporting. The US news media, after all, operate in a more relentless commercial framework, while both the BBC (as a largely non-commercial public broadcaster) and even ITV have a more clearly defined public service remit. However, what is immediately notable about our findings overall is the *similarity* of the forms and pattern of citizen/public representation. This suggests that the *way* news represents citizens is part of a set of well-established journalistic practices that cross the Atlantic (and may, in fact, be even more widespread).

Our press sample was also large – based on 2,720 references to citizen/public opinion (1,697 in the US sample and 1,023 in the British sample) in 1,248 different news articles. It was, however, narrower and more focused in its scope. Since we did not know how many examples of opinion polls we would find in the television sample, we constructed the press sample to focus on opinion polls, using the key words 'poll', 'polls' or 'people think'. It is based on two well-established broadsheets, the *New York Times* in the USA and *The Times* in Britain, and covers two different periods (1st June 2001 to 30th September 2001, and 28th January 2002 to 11th February 2002).

Our aim was not to provide a direct point of comparison with the broadcast sample but to explore certain kinds of representation – notably opinion polls. While our analysis of broadcast news allowed us to capture *every* reference to citizen or public opinion, regardless of the language used, our press sample did not. Our main focus, in what follows, will therefore be on our more comprehensive television sample, apart from Chapter 4, where the focus is on opinion polls.

In both samples we explored a number of variables, the main ones being the following:

- how public or citizen opinion was invoked or represented;
- the section of the public or population referred to;
- the source of the reference to public opinion;
- the placement of the reference in the story, and in relation to other references;
- the subject of public or citizen opinion;
- the political complexion of the statement of or about public opinion;
- the degree of citizen engagement suggested by the reference.

Before we discuss our findings, we should note that designing a coherent coding frame was a significant methodological challenge for this project, especially in our TV news sample, where references to citizenship and public opinion are often subtle. The coding frame was piloted extensively, and repeatedly tested by the three members of the research team to ensure a high level of inter-coder reliability. Most of the material was coded by one main coder, and then tested by the other two members of the research team. On most simple measures (such as the designation or the source of references) agreement between coders was between 90% and 100%. On more complex measures such as the level of citizenship engagement, reliability was initially much lower (around 80%). For this reason, we isolated areas of potential ambiguity, and resolved these each week during project team meetings. While this 'collective coding' approach is unorthodox, we felt it appropriate for the most complex forms of measurement. The coding sheet was amended several times during the early stages of the project, and in each case the entire sample was re-coded accordingly, with checks to ensure at least a 90% level of inter-coder reliability.

While any study is limited by time and scope, what follows is, we hope, a comprehensive analysis of the roles citizens play – for better or for worse – in the main British and the US news media. The next two chapters provide an overview of our main findings. Chapter 2 looks at the main ways in which citizenship is represented or invoked on the news, and the degree to which this is informed by evidence about what citizens think or do. Chapter 3 develops this analysis, exploring the extent to which citizens are seen – or referred to – as active and engaged in politics and public affairs.

We then explore the main forms of citizenship representation in more detail. This begins in Chapter 4 with an analysis of the use of opinion polls. Our focus here is less on technical issues and more on broader questions about the way polls are used, and the forms of citizenship that they signify. Chapter 5 looks at the 'vox pop', which is the only widely used news convention that allows ordinary citizens to enter the 'newsworld'. These are the most conspicuous images of citizenship on the news, and we look at what vox pops tell us about what it means to be a citizen.

While both opinion polls and vox pops are distinct and identifiable, many references to public opinion or to citizens are not. Chapter 6 deals with these rather vague, less precise references, in which journalists – often indirectly – convey assumptions about what citizens think and desire.

Chapter 7 stands alone, and looks at the way in which citizenship and public opinion was invoked during the biggest news story in our time period: the attacks on New York and Washington on September 11th 2001 and the subsequent 'war on terror'. We conclude our analysis in Chapter 8, which reviews our main findings and offers both explanations and recommendations for the future. Our bias throughout is, we hope, uncontroversial. We subscribe to a notion of democracy that values – and depends upon – active and engaged forms of citizenship, and our recommendations are for those who would like to see the news media play a positive role in strengthening representative democracy.

2   Meet the public

There is no clear or well-defined place for an ordinary citizen in the world of news. To enter what we might call the 'newsworld', a 'member of the public' must usually become something *more* than a mere citizen. Often this involves acquiring power or wealth, but it is also a privilege extended to a wider range of people, whether because they are experts, criminals, or victims and witnesses of unusual or significant events. In each case, their citizenship is partly left behind as they are plucked out from the everyday world to offer testimony. They are no longer ordinary citizens, but people who are, whether by accident or design, especially qualified to comment. The news, almost by definition, may be *for* citizens, but it is not about them.

In a society suffused with a robust celebrity culture, it is not just news but television in general that expresses a paradoxical attitude towards citizenship. Many genres, from sitcoms to soap operas, feature 'ordinary people' dealing with citizenship issues, (particularly in Britain) but they do so in a parallel universe: in *our* world the people playing these roles are elevated above the everyday. So, for example, when someone enters the *Big Brother* house they are defined (if rather coyly) as an 'ordinary person' – and yet their very presence in a 'reality' television drama changes their status into something else. In this case, they become celebrities of the emptiest and most tautological kind: they are people who are known simply for being known. As Boorstin once put it: 'the celebrity is a person who is known for his (or her) well-knownness' (Boorstin, 1961).

The boundaries of the newsworld are more rigidly defined, but the paradox of *Big Brother* – whose contestants are simultaneously ordinary and celebrated – is an illustration of the way the rules of media engagement are stacked against the citizen. The principle role for the citizen is not as a participant but as a viewer. Indeed, definitions of 'good citizenship' often involve watching the news, whereby spectatorship becomes a form of civic duty (Ouellette, 1999). It is not so much that citizens are typically excluded from news, simply that they are *not* there because they are voters, members of communities or because they have a stake in the state of the world. They are there because they have experiences, status or knowledge that most citizens do not have.

There are two obvious exceptions to this, two moments when citizens *are* cast simply as citizens. The most routine is the 'vox pop', when reporters gather the views of ordinary people on a newsworthy topic. It is a convention generally associated with television news, although it is also a part of print journalism, as this example from the *New York Times* suggests:

> Not everyone sees the stakes as being so high. Stacey Jaffee, 36, an interior architect who lives in Greenwich Village, said that if she voted at all, she would use her customary method of asking other women in line at her polling place whom they would recommend. Other than that, she did not pay too much attention. 'It's the primary, right?' she said.
>
> (*New York Times*, September 11th 2001)

'Vox pops' provide journalists with easy copy: they are easy to do and easy to watch – and yet their function is unclear. They are there to offer a slice of life, they provide a chance to see what ordinary citizens have to say on a given issue. They are, in this sense, there to represent the ordinary citizen. At the same time, unlike opinion surveys, they represent citizens without the journalistic burden of being defined as necessarily *representative*.

We shall explore this ambiguity later when we look at 'vox pops' in more detail in Chapter 5. Suffice to say, at this point, that the 'vox pop' represents the most obvious 'citizen slot' in news reporting. And while the 'vox pop' vignette may sometimes be intended as a light interlude, it carries the heavy burden of being the place in the newsworld where citizenship is most clearly expressed and defined.

The second way in which citizens can appear as themselves in the news is when they take part in a protest or demonstration. Indeed, the main purpose of such actions is to turn strongly held citizens' opinion into a news event, and thereby put pressure on policy makers to respond. But the news coverage of such events has always been fraught with contradictions. Demonstrations can be seen, on the one hand, to be the epitome of active citizenship and the hallmark of a democratic society. On the other hand, they are often represented as attempts to interfere with civil society, and are implicitly or explicitly seen in opposition to a silent, law-abiding majority.

These contradictions are partly a result of the fact that protests and demonstrations often become more newsworthy if they involve violent incidents or clashes with the police. The protester is thus lurched from the role of citizen to the role of criminal, to being a *threat to* rather than an *expression of* democracy (Halloran, Elliot and Murdock, 1970). But even law-abiding demonstrations are tinged with a faint air of illegitimacy. So, for example, around midday on 4th February 2004, a debate on the Hutton Report in the House of Commons was suspended – for the first time in the Commons since 1987 – due to a non-violent interruption by anti-war protesters. When news of this event was initially reported, Andrew O'Neil, presenter of BBC2's *The Daily Politics*, suggested that it was just a 'blip' in the democratic process, and that the rational world of Westminster was soon to be restored. Citizen expression, in other words, was portrayed as an *interruption* to the democratic process, rather than a part of it.[1]

Similarly, when Stephen Cushion compared the coverage of young people's attendance at a celebration of the England rugby team's 2003 World Cup display with their involvement in anti-war protests earlier that year, he found a striking difference in tone. While commentators excused sport-related truancy, they tended to be rather more disapproving of their involvement in politics. Cushion writes: 'Perhaps the most patronising comment came from Andrew Marr. The BBC political editor quipped at a protest involving young people, "Well, it beats doing your homework" ' (Cushion, 2004).

There are, of course, moments when protesters can be portrayed sympathetically and their arguments seriously addressed. So, for example, the sheer size and the range of people involved in the anti-war demonstrations in February 2003 obliged most British news bulletins to treat the event as a significant citizen intervention in the political process. This was less the case in the USA (Fox News dismissing US protests as 'the usual slogans from the usual suspects'), perhaps because the British protests took place in a context in which polls suggested widespread support for their position.

There are other exceptional moments when citizens make appearances in news, such as the occasion when a woman – Sharon Storer – confronted Tony Blair about the Health Service during the 2001 British general election campaign and became headline news (Brookes, Lewis and Wahl-Jorgensen, 2004). But these moments are rare. Indeed, the publicity given to Sharon Storer was, in part, a function of British reporters' frustration with the slickness of modern campaigns. But citizens are often invoked by journalists (even if they do not appear to speak for themselves) under the rubric of 'public opinion'. Public opinion, after all, is the lurking presence behind all news about politics and public affairs.

While journalists used polls of various kinds during the nineteenth century (Herbst, 1993), it was during the twentieth century that the development of survey research and sampling techniques gave reporters independent and 'objective' information about the nature of public opinion on any given subject. Indeed, opinion polls often become news stories in their own right (Ladd and Benson, 1992; Asher, 1998). So, for example, polls about public attitudes to the 2003 war in Iraq formed an important part of the way journalists saw the conflict (Lewis, 2004).

Whatever we think about opinion polls (and we turn our attention to the use of polls in Chapter 4), they are the dominant form of citizen expression in modern culture. This expression is fairly passive – in which the citizen is told 'don't call us, we'll call you'. They are, at best, blunt instruments for measuring something as dynamic and ephemeral as public opinion. But they are, unlike the 'vox pop' or the 'protester', usually based on representative samples of the citizenry as a whole. And while academics often chide journalists for their misuse and misinterpretation of surveys (Brady and Orren, 1992), polls provide data that are, in many ways, ideal for news reporting. They often deal in the language of simple binaries and are easily understood.

If journalists are used to dealing with polls and surveys, they also make references to public opinion without them. These inferences about the state of public opinion may be based on a reading of polls or their own day-to-day experience (Gans, 1980), and they are often used to put a story into what we might call its 'democratic context'. So, for example, a commentator might refer to the way in which a politician's latest statement or action will be received by the electorate.

Another common – although rather more tenuous – way of invoking public opinion is by making very general inferences about attitudes that exist within the public sphere, without specifying who holds such attitudes or how widespread they might be. This allows journalists to be seen to be speaking *on behalf* of citizens, rather than for themselves. So, for example, a remark may be prefaced with 'some people say that . . .' or 'many people think that . . .', suggesting that debates within the public sphere are taking place, to such an extent that their participants do not need to be identified.

In sum, there are five different and identifiable ways in which citizens are represented in news, which we have defined as follows:

1. *Vox pops*. This is the format that allows 'ordinary citizens' to appear in news bulletins. This category therefore excludes people interviewed because of their expertise, or people who have merely witnessed an event.
2. *Demonstrations or protests*. This involves reference to forms of collective citizen action.
3. *References to public opinion polls or surveys*. This category identifies the use of polls or surveys about public opinion or citizen behaviour.
4. *Inferences about public opinion*. This category involves statements that *infer* something about public opinion in general, without reference to polling data or other systematic evidence.
5. *Unspecified inferences*. This is a wide-ranging category that refers to a *section* of public opinion without reference to polling data or forms of systematic evidence, and without reference either to public opinion in general or an identifiable sub-group.

These categories are, between them, fairly comprehensive, and in our analysis of television news every single representation of or reference to citizens or public opinion was coded under one of these headings. If a news story contained more than one reference to public opinion, these were coded individually, allowing us to be precise in our analysis, and giving us a total of 4,398 references/representations in our television news sample and 2,720 in our newspaper sample. So, how *is* the citizen or the public most often represented in news?

How news represents or refers to citizens

It is often assumed that the main form of public or citizen representation in media and public life is the opinion poll (most of the scholarly work on public opinion focuses on polls – see, for example, Page and Shapiro, 1992; Salmon and Glasser, 1995). Indeed, since there is so little attention paid in the public opinion literature to any other form of citizen representation (such as the vox pop, for example) we expected to find polls dominating references to public expression.

In both Britain and the USA the media regularly commission polls, and the polling industry produces a wealth of data about what people think and feel about a wide array of issues. So, for example, a network like the BBC or CBS News will regularly report on its own polls: 'A CBS News poll out today reflects the growing annoyance. Last month, more than half those sampled were satisfied with government efforts to improve airport security, but that has now plunged to just 37%' (CBS News, 15th November 2001).

What Table 2.1 makes immediately apparent is that our expectations about the prominence of opinion polls in references to *public opinion in general* were completely unfounded. The great majority of references to citizens or public opinion – 97% overall – *do not involve polls or surveys of any kind*. On US television, we found that less than 4% of references to public opinion involve opinion polls, while in Britain it is less than 2%.

Table 2.1 Types of reference to public opinion on television news (n = 4,398)

Type of reference	US television	UK television
Inference to public opinion	42.8%	44.4%
Vox pops	41.4%	38.7%
Unspecified inferences	9.6%	13.6%
Opinion polls	3.6%	1.8%
Demonstrations	2.6%	1.5%

This is, in many ways, a remarkable finding. While polls have been much criticised for their limitations (e.g. Bourdieu, 1979; Salmon and Glasser, 1995; Hauser, 1999; Lewis, 2001) they remain, for all their contrivances, the *most* systematic form of commonly available evidence we have about what people think about the world. Moreover, polling data are abundant, easily available and would seem to be relevant to most news stories about politics and public affairs. None of the other categories in our study – with the possible exception of demonstrations – requires or involves *any* systematic evidence about the way citizens think or feel. Yet all of them *convey an impression* about public opinion. In short, our findings suggest that while television regularly refers to public opinion, it rarely offers any systematic evidence for the claims being made.

If this seems counter-intuitive, it may be partly explained by a degree of constraint placed upon some journalists in their reporting of polls. The BBC, for example, has guidelines about the use of polls which do *not* apply to more vague, unsubstantiated claims about public opinion (Brookes, Lewis and Wahl-Jorgensen, 2004). But we should not over-estimate the influence of such guidelines in day-to-day reporting (the BBC also has guidelines on the use of vox pops, and this does not appear to limit their use) and the reluctance to use polls may also be a function of a tendency to avoid *overt, deliberative* expressions of public opinion which may, from a traditional journalistic point of view, inhibit the coverage of politics – a point we will develop later.

The most common references to public opinion are what we have called *inferences* – claims made *without* reference to supporting evidence. These account for more than four in ten references to public opinion in both countries (it is also the second most common category in our press sample). A typical example of an inference is this reporter's voice-over on ABC News on 12th September 2001: 'This morning, though, priorities were being pushed back into place by Americans in no mood to give terrorists the satisfaction of seeing the nation come apart . . .' In this instance, the reporter acts as a conduit for popular opinion, able to speak on the public's behalf, to instinctively 'know' the public mood. These kinds of inferences also allow the journalist to interpret and explain events or trends, as this example from the *New York Times* about the downfall of Polish politician Lech Walesa illustrates: 'Mr. Walesa's standing in Poland – if not elsewhere in the world – has been battered by what is widely perceived here as his hubris' (*New York Times*, 21st September 2001).

While such claims are often plausible (and *may* be informed by the journalist's reading of opinion polls) they are also impressionistic and involve a degree of poetic licence. It is easy to see, in this context, how conventional wisdom about public opinion may develop even if it has little grounding in empirical evidence. There are a number of instances of this, one of the more clear cut being King and Schudson's (1995) account of how President Reagan was lauded by journalists for his popularity despite consistently *poor* approval ratings in the polling data. Thus while the polls suggested that Reagan was, in his first two years, one the *least* popular presidents in post-war America, Washington correspondents – regardless of their politics – found him likeable and personable and assumed – wrongly – that most Americans shared their impression.

Indeed, it is the media coverage rather than the polling data that endures, and the myth of Reagan as a widely loved president continues to this day (Lewis, 2001). Our findings suggest that the use of inferences about public opinion is so widespread that there may be many more examples of how conventional journalistic wisdom may fly in the face of polling data.

We see an even greater degree of poetic licence in the 'unspecified inferences' category, which carries no obligations about representing the weight or character of public opinion. References of this 'some people say' variety are fairly common, comprising around one in ten references to public opinion on TV news (and, as Table 2.2 suggests, in the press) in both the USA and Britain. As the following example (about proposals to market the image of the USA) suggests, this is often little more than a linguistic device for *rooting* a body of opinion broadly in the public domain:

> Charlotte Beers is the new under-secretary of state for public diplomacy. She created advertising campaigns for Head and Shoulders Shampoo, American Express and Uncle Ben's Rice. It is a controversial appointment. *Some people believe* the US can use the branding principles of advertising to sell a country. *Others believe* it is naive and superficial. We'll look more closely as the campaign develops . . .
>
> (ABC News, 6th November 2001, our emphasis)

While polls are the clearest indicator of public opinion available to journalists, we have suggested that the most identifiable 'citizen slot' on television news is the vox pop. Unlike polls, vox pops are used often on television news – four in ten references to the public (41% in the US and 39% in British news) are vox pops – constituting the second biggest category of references to public opinion.

We shall explore the nature of the vox pop later (in Chapter 5). At this point, it is worth noting that while vox pops *appear* to provide an impression about public opinion, they are rarely used in the context of survey data that might indicate how common the views expressed by these 'people on the street' actually are. Indeed, the BBC guidelines for the use of vox pops make clear that they are *not* a device intended to indicate the direction or weight of public opinion. Whether viewers understand this distinction is quite another matter: we found *very few* instances when the 'unrepresentative' nature of vox pops was specified. On the contrary, the place of vox pops in a story often creates an *impression* that they represent majority opinion – in this example, to convey the impression of a general frustration with the weather.

> The wild winter storm leaves a blanket of snow and ice unusually deep in the South. From the Gulf Coast of Alabama up to the Carolinas and Virginia, eight inches so far in Raleigh, 10 in Richmond.
>
> *Unidentified woman*: 'Richmond and the snow drives me bonkers.'
> (NBC Nightly News, 3rd January 2002)

Examples of *demonstrations* are the least common form of reference to public opinion on television news – constituting less than 3% of the British sample and less than 2% of the US sample. It is worth noting that there were a number of public demonstrations held during the period analysed. The most common examples of this in our study were demonstrations around the 'war on terrorism' and the bombing of Afghanistan – usually in foreign countries – such as this brief reference on US television:

> In Iran, hundreds of thousands filled the streets to show their anger at America on the 23rd anniversary of the Islamic revolution in that country. The crowds were reportedly much larger than last year because people are upset at President Bush calling Iran part of an axis of evil.
> (NBC News, 11th February 2002)

The lack of attention paid to citizen activism is not, perhaps, surprising. Peaceful demonstrators have often claimed that they tend to be ignored by the news media. So, for example, research during the build-up to the 1991 Gulf War found that peace protests and members of the peace movement were almost completely excluded from US television news coverage (Naureckas, 1991). These results add considerable credence to the view that while a presidential or prime ministerial speech is usually considered news – almost regardless of content – moderately sized, peaceful demonstrations are often seen as less significant events.

Overall, these data begin to tell a story that we shall see developed throughout this book. In sum, it is apparent that the *most explicit* forms of citizen expression – polls and citizen activism – are by far the *least common* forms in television coverage. Between them, polls and protests account for only 6% of references to citizens on US television, and only 3% of references on British television. Or to put it another way, 95–97% of references to citizens and public opinion on television news feature vague, impressionistic indicators of public mood or attitude, and are not based on any clear source of evidence.

Two other points emerge from these data. First, while we see small variations between the US and British television, what is more striking is their similarity. As Table 2.1 suggests, both show the same patterns in roughly the same proportions. There are also no significant differences between the various news channels in our sample. So, while there may be differences in the style and content of British and US television news, the assumptions about the way citizens should be represented are shared to a remarkable degree. This may be an indication that they are deeply inscribed within a culture of journalism that stretches across the Atlantic (and, since it seems unlikely that this is purely an English-speaking phenomenon, probably further still).

Second, the kinds of citizen representation favoured by news bulletins are also, potentially, those over which the journalists themselves have most control. Opinion surveys and demonstrations are both, to a degree, independent of the news on which they appear (even if polls are sometimes commissioned by news organisations themselves). While vox pops are very much a part of the newsworld (journalists usually having a fairly clear idea of the kinds of opinions they are looking for), the extent to which inferences and references to the public sphere exist beyond the newsroom is a matter of journalistic judgment.

Our press sample is much less comprehensive and geared towards polls. Accordingly, references to opinion surveys are common in both the *New York Times* and *The Times* samples. Overall, 51% of the references in the press sample were to polls or surveys, and while *The Times* is more likely than the *New York Times* to refer to polls, both appear to use polls regularly and routinely. Both also frequently make inferences about public opinion or references to the public sphere, while demonstrations and protests receive little coverage, especially in the USA.

Table 2.2 suggests that the main difference between the U.S. and British newspapers is the use of vox pops, indicating, perhaps, a difference between the styles of US and British 'serious' newspapers. In the US sample, vox pops are used five times more often than in the British sample. These interviews

Table 2.2 Types of reference to public opinion in the press (n = 2,720)

Type of reference	*New York Times*	*The Times*
Opinion polls	47%	57%
Vox pops	15%	3%
Demonstrations	0.2%	2%
Inferences about public opinion	28%	27%
Unspecified inferences	9%	9%
Letters	1%	2%

with 'ordinary citizens' are often used to flesh out poll findings or act as a substitute for them, as in this story about New York politics:

> John Lorenzo, the father of three children and owner of a Laundro-mat on Jamaica Avenue in Queens Village, said the only thing he really cares about its what the next mayor will do about the city's public schools. 'It's totally out of control,' he said. 'Where are their prior-ities? Now we have a beautiful place just to go and get our drivers' license, but when you go into a school there's no air conditioning, the walls are crumbling. It's falling apart.'
>
> (*New York Times*, September 11th 2001)

This device was used much more sparingly in our British sample, where only 3% of references were of this kind, compared to 15% in the *New York Times*.

Who speaks about whom?[2]

Before we consider who is most likely to make statements about public opin-ion, we shall look briefly at *where* public opinion is represented. Since the bulk of news is domestic in outlook, we would expect the main focus on public opinion to be the same. It is therefore not surprising that our data show that, in both Britain and the USA, public opinion at home is considered more newsworthy than public opinion abroad. In total 78% of references to public opinion are domestic and 22% foreign. Indeed, were it not for the presence of a major international story during this period – that of the attacks on the World Trade Center and the Pentagon and the subsequent war in Afghanistan – the proportions detailed in Tables 2.3 and 2.4 would probably be even more slanted towards domestic opinion.

On television, we also see a notable – if predictable – difference between Britain and the USA, with the USA being more inward-looking, and British news more likely to take note of public opinion elsewhere.[3] While the BBC was particularly likely to refer to public opinion abroad, reflecting its emphasis on

Table 2.3   References to public opinion at home and abroad on television news (n = 4,398)

	At home	Other country	World opinion	Several countries	Europe	Unclear
USA	80.1%	16.5%	0.8%	2.1%	0.5%	0.1%
UK	73.8%	24.4%	1.1%	0.5%	0.1%	0.0%
Total	77.9%	19.2%	0.9%	1.6%	0.3%	0.0%

Table 2.4 Percentage of references to public opinion at home and abroad in the press (n = 2,720)

	At home	Other country	World opinion	Several countries	Europe	Unclear
USA	75.3%	21.4%	0.1%	0.8%	2.3%	0.1%
UK	73.0%	24.6%	0.0%	1.4%	0.9%	0.1%
Total	74.4%	22.6%	0.0%	1.0%	1.8%	0.1%

international coverage (Hargreaves and Thomas, 2002), both the BBC and ITV have more references to public opinion elsewhere than any of the three US networks.

This is, however, a little deceptive, since many of the references on British news to opinion elsewhere focus on the USA, reflecting the dominance of US news in Britain. Indeed, it is remarkable how few references there are to public opinion in Europe – *especially* in British media (despite the easy availability of data). Indeed, the British broadcasters are five times *less* likely to refer to European opinion than the inward-looking US media. There are, by contrast, almost no empirical measures of opinion worldwide, and yet British TV reporters are more likely to refer vaguely to 'world opinion' than to European opinion (even while references to *British* attitudes to Europe are quite common – see Brookes, Lewis and Wahl-Jorgensen, 2004). This finding reflects other recent studies of British television news (see Lewis, Cushion and Thomas, 2004), and suggests that there persists, in the culture of British journalism, an abiding lack of interest in European life.

We see the same pattern in press coverage, with the *New York Times* showing more interest in European public opinion than *The Times* does, although in this sample the US focus on domestic opinion is less pronounced.

When it comes to who speaks – rather than who is spoken about – it is journalists who clearly dominate – the source of 83% of references on television news overall (in this case, with similar proportions for the USA and Britain). While politicians may purport to speak for public opinion, they are not often seen doing so on television, the only other significant voice here being domestic 'experts' of various kinds, who account for one in ten references to public opinion.

Journalists are also the dominant source of statements about public opinion in the press. This is particularly the case for *The Times*, where 90% of the sources of statements about public opinion come from reporters (compared to 81% in the *New York Times*, which is almost twice as likely to quote politicians or experts).

If domestic public opinion gets more coverage than public opinion

Table 2.5   Sources for references to public opinion on television (n = 2,619)[a]

Anchor/ reporter	Politician at home	Expert at home	Military at home	Politician in other country	Expert in other country	Military in other country
83.1%	3.9%	10%	0.3%	1.4%	1.1%	0.2%

a. These data obviously exclude vox pops.

elsewhere, in more than 98% of cases on television, the *sources* of claims about public opinion are domestic. So, even when foreign public opinion makes the news, it is generally conveyed by a domestic expert or reporter.

Apart from the predictably domestic emphasis of news – especially on US television – what emerges here is the degree to which it is common practice for journalists to make claims about public opinion. It is clear that journalists feel an obligation – and an ability – to either speak for or about the public. This is consistent with journalists' self-understanding, which emphasises their role as servants of the public (e.g. Gans, 2003: 1). What is less clear is how aware journalists actually *are* of what citizens think and want. As we have seen, most claims are made without citing supporting evidence. In this context, the process by which journalists make assumptions about public opinion is clearly a matter that merits scrutiny.

What is worrying about these data, given the dominant role journalists play in communicating public opinion, is that most studies of the news media's understandings of public opinion suggest that journalists have little direct interaction with citizens, either directly or through research. Instead, they tend to rely on their own ideas about readers and viewers, impressions that are developed and reinforced within the culture of the newsroom. Gans (1980), for example, found that editors tended to routinely reject feedback in the form of market surveys, letters and phone calls out of a mistrust of statistics *and* of the views represented in these forms of feedback. In their search for audience opinion, editors were much more likely to rely on 'known' groups, such as family members, friends or people in their local communities.

Similarly, Sumpter's (2000) ethnographic case study suggested that journalists construct 'imaginary, local readers' who nevertheless 'often resembled the interests and demographics of the people in the newsroom' (Sumpter, 2000: 338). Indeed, Wahl-Jorgensen's (2002b) work on how journalists discuss the people who write letters to the editor suggests that the culture of the newsroom may create a discourse of disdain for the public. All of this indicates that journalists' inferences about public opinion cannot be taken at face value, but should be understood as culturally constructed ideas, built on the basis of what is often feeble evidence.

In short, journalists frequently invoke the public, and would appear to do so under the cover of journalistic licence. And while opinion polls may be a common part of the news landscape, they appear to play a surprisingly minor role in the news media's coverage of public expression. In the next chapter, we shall examine what kinds of citizenship are invoked under this licence, and what kind of picture the news media paint of popular opinion.

Notes

1. We are indebted to Stephen Cushion for bringing this material to our attention.
2. All the data in this section exclude vox pops, who speak for themselves.
3. Chi-square tests suggest that the differences between the USA and the UK are highly significant (0.000) in the 'home', 'other countries' and 'several countries' categories, and somewhat significant (0.084) in the 'Europe' category.

3 How active are citizens in the media?

In Chapter 2, we demonstrated that while television makes frequent references to citizens and public opinion, these tend to be vague and impressionistic, with little recourse to any systematic evidence. In this chapter we explore a question that lies at the heart of our inquiry: how *active* are citizens or the public in the news media? And more broadly, what do viewers and readers *learn* from the media about what it means to be a citizen? In so doing, we will look at what we hear 'concerned citizens' talking about, and how they are positioned on a political spectrum. And we will analyse the extent to which the public is portrayed as the driving force in a democratic society, or alternatively, as passive and disengaged citizens.

The politics of public opinion

We have become used to the idea that, in a modern democratic system, public support is used to confer legitimacy upon political policy. And yet there are still moments that reveal the immaturity of our democracies. It may be more than eighty years since Walter Lippmann expressed scepticism about the ability of a fickle, hedonistic public to make wise democratic decisions (Lippmann, 1922, 1925), but our political language is full of doubts about the democratic ideal. So, for example, Tony Blair's decision to commit British troops to fight a war in Iraq despite massive anti-war demonstrations and a lack of strong public support was lauded in many quarters as a sign of principled leadership. This sentiment was expressed in the *Financial Times* thus:

> The crisis over the past few months has already redefined Mr Blair's leadership. Few accuse him now of being a Prime Minister who sways with the latest focus group or opinion poll. He has been unbending in his belief that dealing with Saddam Hussein is essential to rescue the

> Iraqi people and protect the world from the proliferation of weapons
> of mass destruction.
>
> (*Financial Times*, 18th March 2003)

We should note here that 'leadership' is defined *not* as the ability to express
the popular will, but in direct opposition to it. So, for example, it is often said
that politicians should lead rather than follow public opinion. Citizens, in
this formulation, are no better than the hapless, misguided masses that Walter
Lippmann worried about. Whether or not this view of the world is paternal-
istic or harks back to a feudal yearning for a benevolent dictatorship, of 'good
kings' and enlightened strongmen, it is anti-democratic. This is not say that
there are not many moments when the public *is* misinformed or misguided,
but we should take care to think about who is implicated in this. Even if
ignorance may sometimes be blissful, to be misinformed or misguided is,
from democracy's perspective, undesirable and unhealthy. In well-educated
democracies, the culpability for such a condition rests not with the public,
but with a political leadership or a mass media that created, encouraged or
permitted it.

So, for example, when polls in the USA showed that majorities believed
Saddam Hussein was implicated in the attack on the Twin Towers and the
Pentagon in 2001, this was not because the US citizenry was stupid or inatten-
tive (Kull, 2003) but precisely because they *were* listening to political and opinion leaders who were happy to foster such an idea (Lewis, 2004). Indeed, as
Stephen Kull's analysis suggests, misperceptions are clearly linked to those
information sources – notably the Fox network – most committed to fostering
them.[1]

It is axiomatic, in this context, to say that a democracy depends upon a
well-informed public. This proposition inevitably places a heavy burden upon
the news media, which are the dominant source of information about politics
and public affairs (Hargreaves and Thomas, 2002). Whether it is *fair* to do so is
not the issue; it is simply an acknowledgement of how modern democracies
work.

The plaudits given to leaders who follow their 'principles' rather than the
polls, are, we would argue, either a sign of deep discomfort with the democratic ideal, or else an acknowledgement that we do not live in a healthy
democracy populated by well-informed citizens. And yet, even if public opinion is sometimes treated with a degree of contempt, the democratic ideal
remains central to our political culture. Although Tony Blair received praise for
his 'leadership' and 'unbending belief', his failure to persuade large sections of
the public of his case for war in Iraq in 2003 was generally acknowledged to be
a problem. And there is no doubt that a politician's life is very much easier if he
or she pursues objectives that are *seen* to have public support.

The word 'seen' is important here. Since we do not have government by referenda, political legitimacy is not, most of the time, conferred *directly* by citizens. Apart from elections – which do not involve any clear endorsement of any particular policy – or occasional referenda, public opinion plays no *formal* role in policy decision making. And yet, as we have seen, public or citizen opinion is continually invoked in news reporting. Citizens thereby have an informal role in democratic politics – one that is heavily dependent *on the way they are represented in news media*.

In a political sense, public opinion only really matters when it becomes 'public' (Lewis, 2001). We therefore rely upon reporters to invoke public opinion to hold politicians to account, to point out which policies have public support and which do not. So, for example, a reporter in the USA might ask politicians why they are not devoting greater resources to health and education, since these are the public's two most consistent priorities for increased public spending. Or a British reporter might ask why they are ignoring the public's desire for the railways to be returned to public ownership. We, as citizens, may hold any number of views, but those views will only impinge upon the political process if journalists are aware of them and choose to draw attention to them.

In Chapter 2, we showed that citizens themselves have little control over this informal process. So, for example, proactive expressions of public opinion that take place in the real world are rarely covered – protests and demonstrations only play a minimal role in the media representation of public opinion. At the same time, other outlets for citizen expression in the news media – such as letters to the editor or emails to news programmes – are still limited, especially in mainstream news programmes. As we have suggested, a citizen's relationship with news media is still very much a matter of 'don't call us, we'll call you'. The initiative, in most cases, rests with the journalist or the pollster rather than with the citizen.

The representation of public opinion is, like any other aspect of news, a question of selection and interpretation. This requires us to ask which aspects of public opinion are chosen by journalists to be worth reporting. Given the wealth of available data, do those 'public opinions' that receive news coverage conform to any particular patterns or framework? Or are they chosen pragmatically to produce a fairly random selection of 'public opinions'?

This, in turn, raises the key question of how public opinion is represented in ideological terms. In short, *is citizen opinion more likely to be represented if it leans to the left, the centre or to the right?* To investigate this question, every reference to (or representation of) public opinion in our study was coded in one of four categories: views that could be broadly labelled as on the left, views that could be broadly labelled as on the right, views that indicate a centrist or mixed ideological view, and views that do not indicate any clear ideological preferences.

There are, of course, no precise definitions about what constitutes a right-leaning or left-leaning opinion. These can be contested terms, and while political parties can sometimes cohere around an ideological position, the embrace of aspects of market economics by traditionally left-leaning parties (such as the British Labour Party or the US Democrats) has complicated ideological perceptions. None the less, we are still able to use a broad ideological continuum to describe this process. Thus we can say, as many have, that Tony Blair has pushed the Labour Party to the right. In so doing, we can identify a set of broad principles that can be associated with the right or left.

Generally speaking, we have categorised opinions as left-leaning or right-leaning as follows:

Left-leaning opinions are those that favour:

- high levels of government spending on public services;
- regulating private enterprise to achieve socially desirable goals;
- any measures designed to redistribute wealth towards those on lower incomes;
- liberal attitudes towards personal or 'normative' behaviour (such as gay rights or abortion), or towards issues of crime, security and immigration;
- foreign policies that involve multilateral institutions (like the UN), and stress the peaceful resolution of conflict, environmental protection and the reduction of global inequalities.

Right-leaning opinions are those that favour:

- privatisation, decreasing taxes, and lower government spending on public services;
- deregulating private enterprise and support for neo-liberal market economics;
- the rights of individuals to accumulate property and wealth;
- conservative attitudes towards personal or 'normative' behaviour, or towards issues of crime, security and immigration;
- foreign policies that stress the importance of military spending and that favour national interests over multilateral institutions and agreements.

So, does television news show public opinion leaning to the right, centre or left, or does it maintain a steadfast neutrality? What is most striking about Tables 3.1 and 3.2 is the degree to which, on both US and British television, citizens are represented as *non-partisan*. In our sample overall, 90% of references to public opinion in the USA and 95% of references in Britain expressed no clear political leaning at all – whether to the right, the left, mixed or centrist. Remarkably, this is even the case with demonstrations. Although they are

Table 3.1   The political leaning of public opinion in US television news (n = 2,880)

	Left wing	Right wing	Mixed	Unclear	Total
Opinion polls	7.7%	29.8%	0.0%	62.5%	100%
Inferences	0.5%	8.4%	0.1%	91.1%	100%
Vox pops	1.4%	6.5%	0.1%	92.0%	100%
Demos	5.3%	3.9%	1.3%	89.5%	100%
Unspecified inferences	1.4%	7.2%	1.1%	90.2%	100%
Whole sample	1.4%	8.1%	0.2%	90.3%	100%

Table 3.2   The political leaning of public opinion in British television news (n = 1,518)

	Left wing	Right wing	Mixed	Unclear	Total
Opinion polls	14.3%	14.3%	0.0%	71.4%	100%
Inferences	0.1%	4.6%	0.6%	94.7%	100%
Vox pop	0.0%	2.6%	0.0%	97.4%	100%
Demos	4.3%	8.7%	0.0%	87.0%	100%
Unspecified inferences	0.5%	5.3%	0.5%	93.7%	100%
Whole sample	0.5%	4.2%	0.3%	95.1%	100%

often associated with the political left, only around one in twenty references in our sample overall made this association.

In both countries, vox pops are routinely apolitical, especially on British television news, where 97% of those citizens used are shown saying nothing of any clear political orientation. So, for example, in the following excerpt from ABC News, a woman is seen as telling us that 'people are worried':

> Since the terrorist attacks, a five-mile no-fly zone has been set up around the depot, which is now cut off by barricades and guarded by more than 100 National Guard troops.
>
> *Unidentified woman*: 'I think people are worried, more than they – they're showing.'
>
> Worried because one incident could more than wipe out an entire town. The danger doesn't come in an envelope. It is already here. Neal Karlinsky, ABC News, Umatilla, Oregon.
>
> (ABC News, 5th November 2001)

While such sentiments could be – and have been – exploited by politicians to favour certain policies (notably the increases in military spending, the 'Patriot

Act' and the invasions of Afghanistan and Iraq), it is, in itself, apolitical. The greater use of vox pops with ideologically recognisable opinions in the USA is entirely accounted for by right-leaning opinions. Thus when citizens are allowed time to speak their minds on US news, right-wingers out-number left-wingers by four to one.

Our finding suggests that the most overtly political form of citizen representation is the opinion poll. This is, perhaps, not surprising, since this is largely what we imagine public opinion polls are there for. Yet even in this case, only 36% of polls referred to in the USA and 29% in Britain convey a message that indicates an identifiable position. So, for example, the following poll featured on CBS News indicates how people are feeling, without suggesting any political course of action:

> And this year it seems the Bronx Bombers represent much of America. A new CBS News/*New York Times* poll shows 33% of the public's pulling for the Yankees, just 24% for the Arizona Diamondbacks. But perhaps the most telling statistic: 42% don't really care. That's the odd thing about this World Series; in so many ways it couldn't mean less, and it couldn't mean more.
>
> (CBS News, 30 October 2001)

In sum, notwithstanding the difficulty of categorising opinions on an ideological scale, the extent to which non-partisan opinions dominate across the board is remarkable.

One explanation for this is that the range of *apolitical* opinions represented in our sample is enormous, from polls about women's handbags to views about celebrities. And yet, as Table 3.3 indicates, most of the issues on which citizens are most often shown (or referred to) expressing themselves – such as terrorism, crime and transport – are *clearly in the political domain*. So, for example, in an item on NBC News about the euro, a woman makes an observation as a tourist, rather than overtly contributing to the political debate about the Single European Currency:

> A single currency devised to streamline life for Europeans, and it will make it easier for American tourists in Europe as well. Only one calculation in so-called Euroland:
>
> *Unidentified woman*: It will take the mystery out of the exchange rates as you move from place to place.
>
> (NBC News, 31st December 2001)

The apolitical nature of references to public opinion cannot, therefore, be explained by an excess of human interest or celebrity news – *what we see here are citizens being apolitical about manifestly political issues*.

Table 3.3   Main topics engaging public opinion on US and UK television news

US TV subject (n = 2,880)	% of citizen references on US TV	UK TV subject (n = 1,518)	% of citizen references on UK TV
Mood after September 11th	16.0%	Health	12.1%
Terrorism	10.3%	Event in world of sport	7.8%
Military attacks on Afghanistan	8.3%	Crime	6.3%
Anthrax	5.8%	Consumption/ shopping	5.7%
Consumption/ shopping	5.3%	Military attacks on Afghanistan	5.7%
Fear of flying	4.5%	Railways	4.9%
Economy	3.8%	Northern Ireland	3.9%

In many cases we found that this was because public expression generally stops short of overt political opinion, which is a realm left to experts and politicians, who are thereby given a great deal of freedom to interpret public expressions as they wish. So, for example, a routine report on levels of consumer confidence might be *interpreted* by politicians or parties as support for their economic policies: 'An ABC News poll released today shows consumer confidence holding steady since September 11th. And anecdotal evidence from around the country suggests people are spending again' (ABC News, 2nd October 2001). But, as this example illustrates, members of the public themselves are not seen offering any such analysis or interpretation. And even though people themselves *might have* specific and verifiable views about economic policy, this is an issue left for politicians to debate.

There is a sense here that ordinary citizens are portrayed as almost child-like: they are seen to have moods, experiences and emotions, but they are rarely seen making forays into a deliberative public sphere. In the coverage of the war on terrorism, for example, we heard a great deal about people's fears, but very little about what they thought about relevant foreign or domestic policy. The following example is fairly typical:

> In America's proud, tall buildings, from the Empire State on Manhattan, now New York City's biggest, to Chicago's Sears Tower, tallest in the country, a feeling that landmarks may not be the safest places to work.

Ms Tanya Kukla (Chicago): 'Once we go into actual war, I don't want to be near this building at all.'

(NBC News, 18th September 2001)

Both pro-war and anti-war groups might interpret this woman's reaction in various ways, but what *she* actually thinks about her government going to war remains a mystery. All we know is that she feels nervous. The emotional nature of public opinion in news about terrorism is discussed in more detail in Chapter 7.

British news often features or refers to members of the public unhappy with public services – but we very rarely hear that people want, for example, more public money put into those services – even when polls consistently suggest that this is the prevailing opinion. We shall return to this point shortly, when we examine the degree to which citizens are seen as engaged in politics and public affairs.

When citizens *are* heard expressing a view, it tends to be on the right rather than the left. Indeed, in both cases, the proportion of left-leaning opinions represented is tiny – 1.3% in US news and 0.5% in British news. Perhaps more surprisingly, mixed or middle-of-the-road opinions are even less common. And while there is certainly no abundance of right-leaning opinions either – 8.1% in US news and 4.2% in British news – they considerably outweigh all other political opinions. Thus in both Britain and the USA, 84% of politically inflected opinions are right-leaning.

In the USA, this imbalance is reflected in every kind of manifestation of public opinion except demonstrations. Opinion polls featured on US network news, for example, run more than five to one in favour of conservative opinions, with no instances of mixed opinions at all. While it could be argued that public opinion in the USA *does* incline to the right rather than the left, a number of careful studies of US public opinion contradict this (e.g. Page and Shapiro, 1992). While Americans often lend support for abstractions like 'free enterprise' and 'small government', they often tend to favour left-leaning policies on a whole range of specific issues, such as public spending on health and education, the environment, gun control and multilateralism (Kull, 2004).

It could be argued that our data simply reflect the fact that this was a period in which the September 11th attacks and the war in Afghanistan pushed US public opinion to the right on the most newsworthy issues – as the following example, indicating the willingness of Americans to support extensive military action, suggests:

> In addition, the military campaign could be aimed at the Afghanistan ruling party, the Taliban, for harboring bin Laden. Such an effort would require a military commitment the Clinton White House

would not make, and a willingness to accept a large number of American military casualties. After yesterday's devastating terrorist attacks,
former General Norman Schwarzkopf says it's a sacrifice the American
people are willing to make.

(NBC News, 12th September 2001)

However, while it is true that, in our sample, citizen opinion on terrorism (or
issues related to terrorism) was much more likely to be portrayed as on the
right rather than the left, the great majority of references to the public's view
of terrorism – 92% – could not be classified on an ideological spectrum. If we
remove terrorism-related opinions from our sample altogether, the ratio of
right to left opinions in our US sample does not change significantly (the
percentage of left-wing opinions rises marginally from 1.4% to 1.5%, while the
proportion of right-wing opinions remains at 8.1%). So, for example, in a CBS
News story about teachers taking strike action, the public are represented as
overwhelmingly hostile:

That feeling apparently goes beyond the administration in this afflu-
ent district . . . Mary Spatz teaches at an elementary school of 600
kids. She's counted just four parents who've offered support.

(CBS News, 5th December 2001)

What the US news media are thus reflecting is a stereotypical *image* of a
generally conservative American public. This pattern of bias in US news coverage has been found in previous studies, which show that media coverage of
public opinion in the USA reflects the centre-right bias of the political class,
rather than the more diverse inclinations of the public at large (Lewis, 2001).
Paletz and Entman (1981), in particular, have described how the US media tend
to portray public opinion as more conservative than the polls would suggest.

This is reflected in the media use of ideological labels, the term 'liberal'
being generally associated with elites, while ordinary working-class, blue-
collar Americans are typically described as conservative (Lewis, 2001: 91). Our
data suggest that the US news media are simultaneously informed by and
reinforcing the stereotype of the 'average Joe' from middle America – a figure
who more authentically expresses 'real America' than the effete 'metrosexuals'
living on the east or west coasts. The familiarity of this stereotype allows journalists to comfortably identify and express this voice, as in this example of
support for the 'Patriot Act' on ABC News:

. . . right now the calls for action are drowning out the second
thoughts. As one veteran of World War II put it today, if you have to
violate freedom to protect the masses, go ahead and do it.

(ABC News, 21st September 2001)

The stereotype of a conservative US electorate is widely held. So, for example, after the presidential election of 2004, which President George Bush won with just 51% of the vote, Gavin Hewitt, for BBC News, was able to assert confidently: 'this remains a deeply conservative country' (BBC 10 O'Clock News, 3rd November 2004), and to ascribe Bush's victory to the preponderance of conservative values in the USA. It is, in fact, fairer to say that Bush won *despite* holding a range of views to the right of the majority of Americans. So, for example, research by Stephen Kull for the Program on International Policy Attitudes at the University of Maryland revealed that most Bush voters surveyed supported the global treaty on climate change, the treaty to ban landmines and a range of other multilateral initiatives, all of which Bush opposed. And yet most assumed that Bush *also* supported these measures (Kull, 2004).

As we have suggested, the existence of such a mythic figure is based on only a very selective reading of the polling data. The fact that it persists is partly because, as Gans (1980), Sumpter (2000) and Wahl-Jorgensen (2002b) have suggested, journalists are more likely to rely on intuitive, peer group accounts of public opinion than a thorough analysis of the social scientific data. However, like many myths, it is also derived from a partial truth – in this case, the polling data that suggest that 'ordinary' Americans tend to be more conservative on certain social or lifestyle issues than their more liberal, upper-middle-class counterparts. The fact that working- or lower-middle-class people in the USA also tend to be *more progressive* on economic and social justice issues (Harrigan, 1993) is easier to ignore in the US media's coverage of politics, because it is often social issues – from stem-cell research to gay rights – that are seen to define political divisions (Lewis, 2001).

An example of one of the few left-leaning opinions featured on US news followed the Enron scandal, when polls suggested a high degree of support for tighter business regulation:

> Did Enron executives do wrong? Those paying close attention say yes – 78% . . . And nearly as many, 77%, think the executives should not have been allowed to sell their stock while preventing workers from selling theirs.
>
> (CBS News, 1st January 2002)

A careful reading of polls shows that this kind of attitude is not unusual. Americans may be against the *idea* of 'big government', but on specific issues where the community or social interest is clear, they tend to favour regulation. What is unusual, apparently, is for such views to make the news.

The British television news media are less inclined to show opinions of *any* political hue. In terms of opinion polls, they appear to succeed in a remarkable display of balance (with 14.3% of polls on the right and 14.3% on the left). Table 3.3 indicates that it is in the less systematic articulations of citizen opinion that a small but clear right-wing bias appears to creep in. This is most obviously the case when *journalists themselves* refer to public opinion (the 'inferences' categories) without the evidence of polls, demonstrations or vox pops – as in the following example about illegal immigration:

> [the decision not to the take train driver to court is] . . . not going to play particularly well with many people in the South-East constituency who already feel illegal immigrants are getting in too easily . . . and not well with lorry drivers either . . .
>
> (BBC 6 O'Clock News, 4th February 2002)

Or in this story on anti-terrorism laws: 'MPs do not like it, but feel the public might actually welcome laws that are seen as tough' (BBC 6 O'Clock News, 19th November 2001).

While these statements are highly plausible, we rarely see similar inferences in British news suggesting a left-leaning body of opinion. Indeed, based on our data, when reporters make references to politically inflected public opinion they are *more than sixteen times more likely to be right-wing than left-wing*. What this suggests is that many British journalists share with their US counterparts an instinctive sense that domestic public opinion tends to be conservative.

Thus it is that, with remarkable symmetry, a mythic 'middle England' has emerged, with many of the features that characterise the stereotype of 'middle America'. In both cases, its inhabitants are seen as patriotic, parochial, with traditional values and as politically moderate to conservative. Thus when journalistic speculation about public opinion *does* link citizens with political ideology, it is invariably tinged by this image of 'middle England'.

And yet if the bias is the same, its origins are not. The history of British politics is bound up with traditions of working-class support for socialist parties, with ideological divisions that tend to focus on structural and economic issues. The stereotype of 'middle England' is, in part, a form of psephological shorthand, based on the more marginal constituencies between the more conservative south and Labour's northern and Celtic heartlands. Quite why this area has become associated with politics that lean to the right is less clear.

Part of the explanation, we would suggest, stems from the overtly political role played by the popular press. Since British tabloids are more likely to lean to the right, it is easy to see how journalists may well assume that popular right-leaning papers like *The Sun* and *The Daily Mail* are, somehow or other, reflecting their readers' views. Indeed, the role of *The Daily Mail* – the dominant mid-market tabloid – has been pivotal in attempting to cast 'middle England' in its own conservative image. Thus it may be that journalists look to the press in Britain rather than to opinion polls as an indicator of the public mood. If this gesture makes for rather poor social science, it may well reinforce the power of conservative newspaper proprietors to set the news agenda.

So, while we often hear a mythic 'middle England' invoked as a barrier to progressive policies, there is no progressive equivalent. The large part of the British public that wants to limit privatisation in public services, see the wealthy pay a larger share of the tax burden and spend more on health and education, has no moniker in journalistic parlance.

The left-leaning inclinations of public opinion on public services might be pertinent, for example, when discussing the privatisation of the railways, which was the sixth most popular topic associated with public opinion in our British sample. Yet despite clear majority support in polls for bringing the railways back into public ownership (around 60–70% support, according to polls by MORI and ICM), among the dozens of stories on this issue in our sample we found *no* indications that there might be public support for the re-nationalisation of the railways.

Finally, it is worth noting that examples of ideologically mixed or centrist public opinion are surprisingly rare on television news in both countries – less than three references in a thousand indicate that people are middle of the road, mixed or divided about which political direction to follow. The following is one of the few examples indicating ambiguity in public opinion:

> The biggest holdout is Britain, which hasn't adopted the euro, but is watching it very closely. There's a fierce debate here about whether to join the common currency or to keep the strength and sovereignty of the pound, not to mention the picture of the queen.
>
> (ITV 6.30pm News, 10th December 2001)

While this news item does not explicitly tell us who is involved in this debate, there is an implication here that citizens are actually debating a political issue. This is, in terms of TV news coverage, almost unheard of. As we shall see shortly, citizens may feel, desire or complain, but they do not, on the whole, discuss the merits of political ideas – not, at least, on television news.

Our press sample is less comprehensive, and is, on this issue, constrained by the particular stance of the newspapers involved. The *New York Times*, despite its establishment credentials, is generally regarded as leaning towards east coast, liberal and Democratic values, while *The Times*, like most Murdoch titles, generally leans to the right. These political leanings are, to an extent, reflected in the way they represent public opinion. And yet even a paper on the mainstream centre-left in the USA – serving a largely metropolitan, Democratic readership – is a little more likely to represent public opinion as on the right rather than on the left (albeit to a lesser extent than network television news).

The pattern of representation in the *New York Times* is similar to British

Table 3.4   The political leaning of public opinion in the *New York Times* (n = 1,697)[a]

	Left wing	Right wing	Mixed	Unclear	Total
Opinion polls	15.8%	12.6%	4.1%	67.5%	100%
Inferences	5.5%	12.2%	1.4%	80.9%	100%
Vox pops	4.3%	11.0%	0.4%	84.3%	100%
Demonstrations	50.0%	25.0%	0.0%	25.0%	100%
Public sphere	4.7%	8.8%	0.7%	85.8%	100%
Letter	22.2%	22.2%	0.0%	55.6%	100%
Whole sample	10.3%	12.0%	2.5%	75.3%	100%

a. The number of references to demonstrations in the sample is so small that, in both samples, the percentages are not meaningful.

Table 3.5   The political leaning of public opinion in *The Times* (n = 1,023)

	Left wing	Right wing	Mixed	Unclear	Total
Opinion polls	9.1%	12.0%	3.6%	75.3%	100%
Inferences	2.2%	12.3%	0.7%	84.8%	100%
Vox pop	0.0%	17.1%	0.0%	82.9%	100%
Demonstration	36.8%	0.0%	0.0%	63.2%	100%
Public sphere	0.0%	3.1%	1.0%	95.8%	100%
Letter	0.0%	0.0%	0.0%	100%	100%
Whole sample	6.5%	11.0%	2.4%	80.2%	100%

television news. The representation of opinion polls is fairly evenly balanced between right and left, while the more impressionistic representations of public opinion lean more unevenly to the right. We see a similar pattern in *The Times*, although the rightward bias of the impressionistic account of public opinion is even more emphatic.

The proportion of politically inflected opinions in both newspapers is higher than in our television sample – 25% in the *New York Times* and 20% in *The Times*, compared with 10% and 5% on US and British television. This is partly a product of the over-representation of opinion polls – the most politically inflected form of public representation – in the press sample.

Levels of citizen engagement

Thus far, our findings suggest that when public opinion *is* shown as overtly political, the news media favour right-wing opinions over those to the left or the middle of the road. This bias – in both the British and the US media – is, we would argue, often a product of impressionistic accounts of public opinion made by journalists themselves. There is nothing necessarily deliberate or conscious about this; journalists are simply favouring stereotypes about public opinion rather than reflecting the polling data.

However, this rightward slant should not eclipse the most striking aspect of our findings, whereby *any* political opinion – either right or left – is notable by its absence. Indeed, our overall findings thus far suggest that while public opinion is often referred to on a variety of issues, the form it takes favours vague, second-hand accounts rather than more explicit expressions (like opinion polls or demonstrations), and is routinely apolitical.

In order to allow us to develop this analysis, we assessed the *degree of political engagement* suggested by each reference to or representation of public opinion. This involved devising categories that would allow us to determine the *nature* of citizen expression: did it involve a statement about people's experience of the world, for example, or did it constitute a more deliberative engagement in the public sphere?

This is a complex question, and, after much discussion and experimentation, we developed five broad categories of citizen engagement. These can, broadly speaking, be seen as a continuum between the active, deliberative and engaged citizen at one end, and the more passive, apolitical citizen at the other. They are as follows:

1. **Citizens making proposals.** This represents the most active form of citizenship, whereby citizens or the public are shown to take a position on an issue that implies some form of action. This means, in practice, citizens making suggestions about what should be done in the world, whether by government, the corporate world or by their fellow citizens. While this is our most deliberative category, we did not set the bar too high in identifying it. It might involve nothing more elaborate than people saying that more public money should be spent to improve schools, that businesses should do more to protect the environment, or that parents should teach their children not to drop litter. Any such suggestion was coded as a citizen making a proposal.

2. **Citizens responding to politicians.** This category also involves people expressing overtly political views, although it is more reactive, the public merely giving – or failing to give – consent or support for the policies or actions of political leaders. It also *tends* to be less policy specific (unless it involves a response to a specific party policy), including, for example, 'horserace' opinion polls or reactions to a politician's performance, behaviour or actions.

3. **Citizens commenting on an issue/event/group without making proposals for action.** This category shows citizens or the public as part of the public sphere *without being deliberative*. This includes any comment on events,

social issues or social groups – such as the state of the health service, working-class people or race relations – that give *no indication of what action should be taken*. We might, for example, see a vox pop saying that the health service is in a mess, without the interviewee saying what they think might be done about it. In short, this type of citizen engagement involves *commentary* rather than *advocacy*, and leaves the world of action, policy and politics to others.

4. **Citizens speaking about personal experiences or as consumers.** This is another non-deliberative category, but one in which citizens speak *as individuals or consumers* rather than as members of a public sphere. So, for example, we may hear about someone complaining that their train was late or that they are scared of flying, without locating themselves in a broader public or suggesting what consequences might follow. We have included references to 'consumer confidence' in this category: while these *can* be more deliberative, they clearly define people as consumers rather than as citizens.

5. **Citizens speaking about sports, celebrity or entertainment.** This category is, almost by definition, apolitical and consumerist. This is not to say that opinions about such topics are *necessarily* apolitical, simply that all the references listed in this category have no obvious civic or political connotations.

Table 3.6 shows, in detail, how these categories were broken down across the whole television sample. What is immediately apparent is that *instances of fully engaged citizens* – making proposals about the world – *are fairly rare on television news*. This is the case in both the USA and Britain, at 5% and 4% of references respectively. So, for example, ABC News, following the September 11th attacks, showed a woman urging her fellow citizens how to behave:

> *Unidentified woman*: 'I think it's important to show our support right now. Even though we're not in New York or Washington, DC, our home was attacked.'
>
> (ABC News, 13th September 2001)

By doing so, she is more engaged in the public sphere than 95% of citizens on television news.

When they are made, most citizen proposals are, as we might expect, directed at government, while citizen proposals about the corporate world are very rare indeed, accounting for 1 in 200 references.

More common – although still only accounting for 17% of references overall – are citizen responses to politicians, whether in reference to their words, deeds, character, record or general persona. In other words, when citizens are seen expressing a view, that view is most likely to be expressed through support for or disapproval of their elected representatives. The following example is fairly typical: a range of issues are mentioned (the 'war on

Table 3.6 Levels of citizen engagement on US and UK television (n = 4,398)

Proposals to government	3.1
Proposals to corporate world	0.5
Proposals to fellow citizens	0.7
Total – citizens making proposals	**4.3**
Ranking of party/politician performance on specific issue	0.0
Support of/opposition to party or government policy	9.1
Approval/disapproval of politician's behaviour/actions	2.3
Approval/disapproval of politician's handling of an issue	0.5
Other responses to political events/actions	3.7
Horse race/elections	0.8
Apathy, cynicism or lack of engagement towards politics	0.4
Total – citizens responding to politicians	**16.9**
Discussing social issue/event, no clear proposal	18.6
Discussing own social group, no clear proposal	4.2
Discussing other social group, no clear proposal	6.0
Appeal to government, no clear proposal	0.3
Appeal to corporate world, no clear proposal	0.0
Appeal to fellow citizens, no clear proposal	0.1
Sense of duty to fellow citizens	0.6
Ranking of concern about an issue	0.3
Emotional response to specific issue/event, no clear proposal	17.3
Vague public mood, no clear proposal	1.1
Total – citizens commenting on issue/event/group without proposals	**48.5**
Private individual speaks about personal experience	23.1
Consumer confidence	2.0
Total – citizens speaking about experiences or as consumers	**25.1**
Citizens speaking about sports, celebrity or entertainment	**5.2**
Total	**100**

terror', the economic recession and unemployment), and while polls suggest that many people have opinions about such issues, the only expression of public opinion we are given is the vague barometer of President Bush's approval ratings:

> It was no ordinary day here in the nation's capital, summer warm in the dead of winter. It is no ordinary time in America. The nation is at war against terrorists and in an economic recession with unemployment rising. Against that backdrop and riding very high in popularity polls, President Bush comes here to the Capitol tonight to deliver his

first official State of the Union address and lay out his ideas for trying to meet the many challenges facing the United States.

(CBS News, 29th January 2002)

This form of public expression is at its most engaged when in response to a specific government policy, as in these examples:

And tonight there's a total news blackout from the Gaza Strip where both Israel and the Palestinians are facing a rising tide of Arab protest in response to those American military air strikes.

(NBC News, 9th October 2001)

An ABC News Washington Post poll today finds that most Americans support the various law enforcement measures the government is taking in the campaign against terrorism. Fifty-nine percent are in favor of military tribunals, 86% say the government's detention of hundreds of people is justified.

(ABC News, 28th November 2001)

In other words, citizens are seen as deliberative, but only in the context of an agenda set by politicians. Public opinion is thereby seen as flowing from the top down rather than from the bottom up.

The most common ways in which citizens are shown, however, come lower down the hierarchy of citizen engagement. Almost half the references to public or citizen opinion involve comments about a social group or issue: observations about the world that offer no clear recommendations or proposals. So, for example, in an NBC story about aggressive and competitive parents at games, we are told by a high school hockey coach that:

They're in the kids' faces as soon as they get off the ice. They're in the coaches' faces as soon as they get off the ice. I mean, you go to the rinks now where they actually have gates that separate the parents from the players and the coaches.

(NBC News, 4th January 2002)

This citizen commentary often involves an emotional response to issues or events – something that characterised references to public opinion in the week and months after the September 11th attacks:

In small towns and big cities, Americans are wondering how long this fight will last and whether it will prove conclusive. You can hear frustration and even impatience from far away South Dakota.

(ABC News, 21st September 2001)

> People are scared, especially parents on Halloween.
>
> (NBC News, 30th October 2001)

> The tragedy and trauma greatest for New Yorkers, so psychiatrists say it's no surprise that with the holidays upon us they show the nation how to heal.
>
> (NBC News, 29th November 2001)

Indeed, just over one in six references to public opinion involve these kinds of emotional responses. This is *not*, we should stress, the purposeful passion of commitment to an idea or a cause; it is reactive and undirected, there to be interpreted or exploited by more powerful voices.

Even further down the scale of citizen engagement are individuals shown or described speaking about their own personal experiences. While these experiences may be connected to broader social issues or political policy, this is done by others – typically experts, reporters or politicians. About a quarter of references overall are in this category which, implicitly or explicitly, represents the public as consumers rather than citizens:

> Sara Deats is confused and angered by her monthly phone bill. The recreation director cannot understand almost a dozen extra fees on her monthly statement from MCI.
>
> *Ms Sara Deats*: 'I wonder, am I being overcharged? This sure seems like a lot to be making as few phone calls as I am.'
>
> Millions of long-distance users are wondering the same thing. The Consumers Union report says six years after deregulation, bills are confusing. And prices for long-distance service are going up.
>
> (ABC News Tonight, 5th February 2002)

> The bright decorations and the stores stockpiled with merchandise are facing Americans reluctant to spend. At the Willowbend Mall in Dallas.
>
> *Unidentified woman 1*: 'We're mostly just out enjoying the Christmas decorations.'
> *Unidentified man*: 'I don't think there is some of the – the sense of euphoria we used to have.'
> *Unidentified woman 2*: 'We've probably looked at our list at little bit more carefully. It's a little shorter this year.'
>
> (ABC News, 21st November 2001)

Despite the generally apolitical representations of citizenship on television news, it is notable that only 5% of references to the public involve overtly apolitical subjects, whether attitudes to sport, entertainment, celebrity or lifestyle. In other words, the apolitical, disengaged and non-deliberative style of citizenship so common on television news is *not* a product of endless lifestyle polls or public approbation of sports or soap stars. Perhaps surprisingly, as Table 3.7 shows, these kinds of references are noticeably more common on British television.

British television is also twice as likely to feature public responses to politicians, and less likely to show citizens responding to or discussing issues or speaking about their personal experiences. Citizens on British television are, in this sense, more deliberative, and more engaged in political debate – although this engagement is generally portrayed as reactive. This may be a product of the long tradition of public service broadcasting in Britain, which places parliamentary political activity and debate at the heart of news coverage.

As Table 3.8 shows, the same could be said of opinion polls, which are used parsimoniously on television news (only around 3% of citizenship references overall) but which appear to indicate, more than half the time, a level of deliberative political engagement. By comparison, the other – more common – categories suggest less deliberative forms of public expression. The vox pop in particular seems to have become a device for showing people acting as apolitical individuals rather than as people involved in the public sphere – or, to put it another way, the vox pop constructs people as consumers rather than citizens. We shall take this point up in Chapter 5, when we consider vox pops in more detail.

What emerges here is a clear pattern in which the references to citizen or public opinion over which journalists have most control – inferences and vox pops – show citizens as *less deliberative or politically engaged*. Whatever the explanation for this, it has profound consequences for the debate about the widespread citizen disengagement with conventional politics. Put bluntly, if television news wishes to play a positive role here, and to provide more images and examples of an engaged citizenry, journalists need to spend more time

Table 3.7   Comparative levels of citizen engagement on US and UK television (n = 4,398)

Levels of engagement	US	UK
Citizens making proposals	5.3	4.2
Citizens responding to politicians	12.2	25.8
Citizens commenting on issue/event/group without proposals	51.8	40.4
Citizens speaking about experiences or as consumers	28.8	18.1
Citizens speaking about sports, celebrity, entertainment, lifestyle	1.8	11.5

Table 3.8 Comparative levels of citizen engagement in US and UK television news by type of reference to citizen or public opinion (n = 4,398)

	Polls	Inferences	Vox pops	Demos	Unspecified inferences
Citizens making proposals	12.1%	4.1%	5.1%	12.1%	3.9%
Citizens responding to politicians	40.2%	15.2%	11.2%	62.6%	29.0%
Citizens commenting without proposals	22.7%	55.2%	41.7%	23.2%	54.1%
Citizens speaking about experiences or as consumers	23.5%	20.4%	36.8%	0.0%	6.0%
Citizens speaking about sports, celebrity, lifestyle etc.	1.5%	5.1%	5.3%	2.0%	6.8%

covering polls and protests and spend less time on more speculative indicators of public opinion.

Although such an approach would, according to our data, make a decisive difference, it is, in some ways, an easy option. It would fail to address *why* inferences and vox pops tend to suggest more passive, apolitical forms of citizenship – an issue that we shall take up later.

Our newspaper sample focuses much more on the coverage of polls (rather than public or citizen opinion in general). As a consequence, the portrayal of citizens in our newspaper sample is much more deliberative. Table 3.9 opposite shows that nearly 60% of references in our press sample are in one of the two politically engaged categories. Over half of these, however, involve either 'horse-race' polls or the approval/disapproval of politicians – a point we shall address in the next chapter.

Conclusion: news and the apolitical, disengaged citizen

Most broadcasters, policy makers and scholars would agree that television news programmes play a central role in informing citizens in a democratic society. This book is about what viewers learn about themselves, as citizens, if they take seriously the normative responsibility to keep up with the news. The picture painted thus far provides a rather depressing answer. Citizens are, on the whole, shown as passive observers of the world. While they are seen to have fears, impressions and desires, they don't, apparently, have much to say

Table 3.9   Levels of citizen engagement in the press (n = 2,720)

Proposals to government	12.8
Proposals to corporate world	0.5
Proposals to fellow citizens	0.4
Total citizens making proposals	**13.7**
Ranking of party/politician performance on specific issue	0.5
Support of/opposition to party or government policy	4.9
Approval/disapproval of politician's behaviour/actions	11.3
Approval/disapproval of politician's handling of an issue	3.5
Other responses to political events/actions	2.6
Horse race/elections	20.1
Apathy, cynicism or lack of engagement towards politics	2.9
Total citizens responding to politicians	**45.8**
Discussing social issue/event, no clear proposal	10.2
Discussing own social group, no clear proposal	2.5
Discussing other social group, no clear proposal	2.8
Appeal to government, no clear proposal	0.7
Appeal to corporate world, no clear proposal	0.1
Appeal to fellow citizens, no clear proposal	0.0
Sense of duty to fellow citizens	0.0
Ranking of concern about an issue	0.9
Emotional response to specific issue/event, no clear proposal	4.9
Vague public mood, no clear proposal	0.4
Total citizens commenting on issue/event/group without proposals	**22.4**
Private individual speaks about personal experience	11.6
Consumer confidence	2.4
Total citizens speaking about experiences or as consumers	**14.0**
Citizens speaking about sports, celebrity or entertainment	4.0
Total	**100**

about what should be done about healthcare, education, the environment, crime, terrorism, economic policy, taxes and public spending, war, peace, or any other subject in the public sphere. The world of politics, in this sense, tends to be left largely to the politicians and the experts.

What emerges from this analysis, in other words, is that while politicians are often seen telling us what should be done about the world, *citizens are largely excluded from active participation in such deliberations.*

This is, perhaps, not all that surprising. In terms of traditional news values, the 'ordinary citizen' is, almost by definition, generally excluded from news about public affairs. As we have pointed out in earlier chapters, most citizens have no authority, celebrity or expertise, and thus have no obvious *place* in a news story, which is mainly reserved for elite sources and opinions. Yet our political system rests, in theory, on what citizens think about the world (e.g. Benhabib, 1994). And the news *is* replete with references to public opinion, whether it is a political commentator speculating in conversation with a news anchor, or 'a person on the street' responding to a journalist's questions. The problem is that while these references provide a constant backdrop, they remain remorselessly apolitical and passive.

Why is this? It may be, in part, because the active citizen, engaged with politics, can be a difficult creature to deal with on a news service committed to impartiality. This is particularly true when public opinion favours clear policy preferences. If a policy is the subject of debate between political parties, show-ing a majority of citizens clearly taking one side or another makes it more difficult for broadcasters to appear even-handed. This may account for why such issue-based polls are so abundant but so little reported.

But perhaps the most profound obstacle to showing active citizens on television news is the traditional top-down structure of political reporting. Politics on the news is usually about what politicians do, and not necessarily what people want them to do. In the British 2001 election, the issue on which public opinion was most often cited was Europe – even though the same polls showed that most people did *not* regard this as a key issue (Brookes, Lewis and Wahl-Jorgensen, 2004). In short, citizens do not set the agenda.

We shall return to these points, and consider what might be done to address them, in our conclusion. But first, we shall consider in more detail the two most obvious forms of citizenship expression – polls and vox pops – as well as the role of citizens in the coverage of the 'war on terror'.

Note

1. Although Kull's data do not prove that people who had misconceptions did so because they watched Fox News, this is, at the very least, one highly plausible explanation for the link.

4   Reporting opinion polls

Much of the scrutiny of the way opinion polls are reported tends to focus on the degree to which the news media report the technical aspects of polls, such as sample size, weighting, levels of sampling error, and so forth. So, for example, Reed Welch, in a study of the reporting of polls in the *New York Times*, the *Washington Post, USA Today* and the *Wall Street Journal*, found that the US press often failed to give the kind of technical details that a pollster would regard as standard. 'The typical article,' he concludes, 'does not give information on the sample size, when the poll was conducted, methods, question wording, and other "minimal essential information" ' – as defined by the American Association for Public Opinion Research. Indeed, such is the paucity of information, Welch suggests, that a 'reader should dismiss the polls altogether' (Welch, 2002: 113).

Stephanie Larson's study of polls on US network news found that even when broadcasters do refer to sampling error in reporting polls, they proceed to make inaccurate statements about the meaning of the data. In short, they often refer to the 'margin of error' without understanding what this means (Larson, 2003). A number of other studies have found a similarly sloppy reporting of the technical and scientific aspects of polling on which, for some, the poll's credibility depends (Brady and Orren, 1992; Asher, 1998). Indeed, the mainstream polling industry – which is concerned with the technical details of polling – clearly has an interest in distinguishing between polls based on solid sampling techniques and less rigorous, fly-by-night operators.

We do not want to belittle the importance of these criticisms: there is no doubt that polls are routinely misinterpreted because of a failure to appreciate technicalities such as sampling error or differences in methodology. But there is also a danger, here, of missing the bigger picture. There are, we would suggest, three different conditions that constrain the meaning of polling data which have little to do with sampling techniques.

First, while polls and surveys are undoubtedly circumscribed by sampling methods, the more profound limits of polling are conceptual rather than technical. Above all, we need to understand that the conversation between the interviewer and the poll respondent – used to generate tables and percentages – is both atypical and artificial. Most of the exchange that takes place is scripted by someone who is not even present, an absent author who micro-manages the whole encounter, deciding which questions are asked, how they are asked, what information is provided (and what is not), and, in most cases, the precise terms in which the answers may be phrased.

A pollster will claim that he or she represents an objective, impartial voice. However, since language itself is rarely value-free, they cannot escape making assumptions about knowledge and meaning (Lewis, 2001). Moreover, it is *their* voice, rather than the interviewee's, that dominates the conversation. Although it is possible to avoid the more obvious ways to push respondents in one direction rather than another, the pollster cannot help providing the con-text in which responses are given (Zaller, 1992). To ask people whether they would like to see lower taxes is not the same as asking whether they want a tax cut and lower funding for public services. The two propositions may amount to the same thing in practice, but they provide very different contexts for respondents. And yet neither question is more objective or impartial – one simply contains more information than the other.

So, for example, MORI surveys in Britain suggested that there was a volu-minous shift in public opinion towards the war in Iraq in March 2003 (Baines and Worcester, 2003). In mid-March they found only 26% supporting war while 63% opposed it. Just two weeks later, this had turned to 56% support with just 38% opposed – a massive 30% swing towards support for the war. And yet the shift may have been, in part, a function of the script designed by the pollsters. The question in mid-March asked people if they would support a war *if* there was no proof from weapons inspectors that Iraq was hiding weapons of mass destruction (WMD) or without UN backing, while the later question contained no such conditions.

It could be argued that this difference was irrelevant, since the war began without proof of WMD or UN backing (i.e. there was little change in the rele-vant real-world context in which the questions were asked). None the less, for those with uncertain or mixed views about the conflict, the first question offered a way to express doubts about the war in a way the second did not. Moreover, while there undoubtedly *was* a shift in attitude during this period, this did *not* necessarily mean that people had changed their minds, as the reporting of these polls implied. Many people who expressed support during the war may *still* have opposed the decision to go to war, but felt obliged to show support for British troops once war began (there is, in fact, evidence that this was indeed the case – see Lewis, 2004).

Our point here is that too much attention on the technicalities of sampling diverts us away from the more profound contrivances of opinion polling. This is not to devalue polls, simply to say that their limits – and the way we should interpret them – have as much to do with art as with science.

Second, our findings suggest that polls are only a small part of the way in which the news media communicate information about public opinion. Over-all, we found that 97% of statements, inferences or indications about public opinion on television news make no reference to polls at all. To focus all our scrutiny on the failure of the news media to report the *technical* details of polls may be understandable – there are, after all, a clear and verifiable set of facts surrounding polls. But given the small part they play in the news media's portrayal of public opinion, there is a sense in which this scrutiny neglects the great majority of references to public opinion. So, for example, the vox pop is a far more commonplace indicator of public opinion on television news than the opinion poll, and yet it is rarely the subject of comment or study (something we redress in the next chapter).

Third, there is no doubt that journalists often tend to see polls simply as predictions of the likely outcome of an election (Brookes, Lewis and Wahl-Jorgensen, 2004). As such, they see elections as the *true* manifestation of public opinion against which polls are measured. This leads to a range of possible misreadings. Journalists may say that a poll 'got it wrong', even if the margin of difference is within the range of sampling error. But more importantly, the poll cannot precisely predict whether the sample of people voting will be rep-resentative of the electorate as a whole (or even of 'likely voters'). So, if the voting population is disproportionately white and middle class (as it often is) it may be that a poll will, in fact, more accurately reflect the preferences of *the electorate as a whole* than the election itself. The poll, in other words, may be more representative of the electorate than the election.

This may sound bizarre to many journalists, but it is, in social scientific terms, difficult to dispute. It is, in this sense, just as plausible to say that an election may misrepresent public opinion as to accuse a poll of doing so. To put it in more technical terms, elections use sampling techniques that most pollsters would dismiss – the sample of people voting may be huge, but it is neither random nor weighted. This would be true even if the voting apparatus of elections were perfect. And yet the scale of technical irregularities possible in US elections, which use various different methods of registration and voting (many of which are subject to abuse), only compound this point.

But the real problem here is one of intent. Polls are often used during – and between – elections, *not* as a way of increasing the democratic accountability of politicians, but as a way of providing a narrative context for political coverage (Brookes, Lewis and Wahl-Jorgensen, 2004). They tell us who is ahead, who is behind, and allow endless speculation about what candidates need to do to win elections. But if we value polls mainly for their predictive powers – which are inevitably limited in close elections – we are ignoring their main democratic purpose. For all their limitations, polls are uniquely able to tell us something about people's policy preferences – what citizens see as priorities for public spending, for example, or whether they favour the privatisation of public services. To reduce polls to merely providing a commentary on the electoral horse race is to muffle what is already a limited form of public expression.

It would be unfair to hold journalists entirely responsible for the emphasis on prediction over opinion. Most survey organisations are complicit in being judged as prophets rather than opinion surveyors. Thus it is that many polling organisations expend a great deal of energy trying to forecast outcomes, to *predict what the public will do* rather than *describe what they think*. So, for example, instead of focusing on what a representative sample of the public say they want, they will often try to *skew* their samples so that they *misrepresent* the population in the same way that elections do. If voters are disproportionately wealthy and white, samples will be weighted to reflect this bias. Polls are being constructed to predict outcomes, not to provide democratic feedback for the political classes. They are, in so doing, perverting the democratic ideals envisaged by democratic theorist James Bryce, to use polls to ascertain 'the will of the majority of citizens' (Bryce, 1895: 258).

We are, for all these reasons, less concerned with whether or not journalists are faithful to the technicalities of polling. Our main concern here is with *how* polls are used by the news media, and with the messages thereby conveyed. While we have used the television sample as our primary source for most of our analysis thus far (since it provides a comprehensive picture of how public opinion in general is represented), it is in this chapter that our press sample, which concentrates more on polls, will be most useful.

Our TV sample identifies just how rarely polls are used to signify public opinion (we found only 131 of 4,398 references to public opinion on television that refer to polls), but it is too small to paint a clear picture of the *way* polls are used. Our press sample, by privileging polls, is more extensive, containing a total of 1,386 references to polls (804 in the *New York Times* and 582 in *The Times*).

Who's polling who?

Since most news in our sample is national rather than regional, it is, perhaps, not surprising that the news media tend to favour polls based on national, general population samples. Just over half the polls used in the US and UK press sample (53% and 52% respectively) are based on these kinds of polls. Again, as we would expect, the *New York Times* – as a regional as well as a national newspaper – is much more likely to include polls based on regional samples, as in the following example:

New Yorkers now hold a sunnier view of their city and its future than they have held in nearly a quarter of a century, with many crediting Mayor Rudolph W. Giuliani for its improved fortunes. Nonetheless, most say they are not concerned about the pending change of leadership at City Hall, and few are paying much attention to the contest to replace him, according to the latest *New York Times* Poll.

(*New York Times*, 15th August 2001)

As we might expect, US network television has a much more national focus. Most of the polls referred to in our US television sample (80%) thus involve national rather than regional samples – the following example from NBC News being the exception rather than the rule: 'Polls show nearly half of Boston area Catholics want Cardinal Bernard Law, accused of hiding the growing problem [of child abuse], to resign, but he tells parishioners he will not quit' (NBC News, 11th February 2002).

The British media, on the other hand, are more likely to refer to polls based on specific population groups. Four in ten polls in *The Times* refer to an identifiable group, compared to less than one in ten in the *New York Times* (see Table 4.1). If we look at who these groups are, we find both similarities and differences.

In the *New York Times*, the population groups referred to more than once in our sample were, in order of frequency: young people, Democrats or Republicans, women, men, business people, parents, plane travellers, employees and Muslims/Arabs. In *The Times*, by far the biggest population group referred to were Tory Party members/activists (11% of their poll references were of this group), a product of a long-running story about the Conservative Party's leadership, as well as reflecting *The Times's* conservative orientation. The following is a typical example, discussing the relative popularity of Tory Party leadership contenders Ken Clarke and Ian Duncan Smith:

The Conservative dilemma is exposed in full in *The Times* this morning. The MORI poll demonstrates that Mr Clarke retains an

Table 4.1   Who is being polled? Types of samples used in polls covered by television and the press

	US TV (n = 104)	UK TV (n = 28)	US press (n = 804)	UK press (n = 582)
General population	80%	43%	53%	52%
People from specific area	9%	21%	32%	6%
Consumers	6%	11%	5%	2%
Population group	5%	25%	10%	40%

overwhelming lead among the electorate in general and has a clear advantage with the 25% of voters who are Tory supporters. By sharp contrast, however, a survey undertaken by this newspaper among members of the Cambridgeshire North East Conservative Association hints that Mr Duncan Smith is poised for victory.

(*The Times*, 26th July 2001)

Other population groups referred to more than once in the *Times* were, in order of frequency: employees, women, young people, music/film fans, men, doctors and/or nurses, business people, teachers, Labour Party members, pensioners, train travellers, sports fans and Liberal Democrats.

This tells us something about which population groups are most newsworthy. As we have seen, references to public opinion are often *about* people, rather than a form of citizen expression, and the population group most commonly referred to – children and young people – fits this model. Polls featuring children tend to tell us what children do rather than what they think – especially when it conforms to stereotypes about moral decline, as this example from *The Times* suggests:

A THIRD OF PRE-SCHOOL CHILDREN HAVE TV

More than a third of children below school age have television sets in their bedrooms, and one in seven has a video recorder. A survey by the Independent Television Commission found that 36% of under-fours were able to watch programmes in their rooms compared to 21% two years ago. The poll, which also found that 14% of under-fours had their own video recorder, also shows that more than half of under-16s have their own television set in their bedrooms. Peter Ainsworth, Shadow Culture Secretary, said last night that the figures were worrying. 'There is no substitute for a book or a live experience of the performing arts or the countryside,' he said. 'We all know that children of parents who read to them perform better at school. Young children have more imagination than the rest of us and they need to be allowed to create their own ideas. It is an incredible statistic.' The research comes after a recent London School of Economics report found that young people in the United Kingdom spent more time watching television than anywhere in Europe. A poll of 15,000 children aged under 17 across 12 countries found that British youngsters were the most likely to prefer watching television to reading.

(*The Times*, 24th July 2001)

Children are, in this report, described purely in terms of their consumption patterns. The irony here, perhaps, is that while the article bemoans the growth of what are seen as passive leisure activities among children, it treats children simply as consumers, choosing between various options.

Polls featuring women – also common – are rather different, and are often a sub-section of 'horse-race' polls (polls that measure the comparative popularity of politicians and parties), as the following example, about the election for the governorship of New Jersey, indicates:

> The new surveys also identify a sizable gender gap. The Quinnipiac poll gave Mr. McGreevey a 23-point lead among women, while a survey released last Thursday by the pollster Scott W. Rasmussen gave Mr. McGreevey a 2-to-1 lead among women.
>
> (*New York Times*, 4th July 2001)

While the 'gender gap' could apply to polls on any issue, this tends to be used largely in relation to horse-race polls, feeding into stories about the general appeal of candidates to men or women.

While most polls covered by the news media are based on domestic samples, we did find that more than one in five polls in the press refer to populations elsewhere (Table 4.2).

Although a number of academic studies have questioned the ability of journalists to report and interpret polls accurately (see also Krosnick, 1989; King and Schudson, 1995), journalists tend to discuss polls themselves, rather than quote others doing so, while expert opinion is rarely sought. Table 4.3 shows that, in our study, only the *New York Times* quotes others using polls in any number, with 10% of its references to polls coming from politicians or experts. In our television and British press sample, 96% of references to polls are made by reporters.

As we have suggested, journalists often see themselves as a conduit for the public voice – as a bridge between the people and the body politic – and these findings would appear to support that view.

Table 4.2 The proportion of domestic versus foreign polls covered by television and the press

	Home	Abroad
US television (n = 104)	98.1%	1.9%
British television (n = 28)	96.4%	3.6%
US press (n = 804)	78.4%	21.6%
British press (n = 582)	77.0%	23.0%

Table 4.3   Who refers to polls in television and newspaper coverage?

	Journalist	Politician	Expert	Other
US television (n = 104)	96%	3%	1%	0%
British television (n = 28)	96%	4%	0%	0%
US press (n = 804)	88%	6%	4%	2%
British press (n = 582)	96%	2%	2%	0%

What are polls about?

Previous studies have documented the news media's tendency to focus on polls that track the popularity of parties or politicians (Lewis, 2001), especially during election campaigns (Brookes, Lewis and Wahl-Jorgensen, 2004). Our data were collected outside a national election period (apart from some gubernatorial elections in some US states), making horse-race polls less newsworthy. None the less, our study suggests that outside national elections, around a third of the polls used by the press are of this kind (Table 4.4), making horse-race polls by far the most dominant type of poll.

Table 4.4   The proportion of horse-race/approval polls (compared with all other polls) used in the press

	Horse-race	Issue/lifestyle etc.
US press (n = 804)	38%	62%
British press (n = 582)	30%	70%

So while horse-race polls may not be *as* newsworthy outside election campaign periods, they are still used to help structure a long-running narrative about politics. The following extract from a lengthy article from the *New York Times* is fairly typical. Under the headline 'G.O.P. Defends Bush in Face of Dip in Poll Ratings', the report began:

> Stung by recent polls showing that President Bush's popularity is slipping, top Republican Party officials insisted today that the president was in fine shape politically. They said that given the closeness of the election last year no one should expect Mr. Bush to be wildly popular. Gov. James S. Gilmore III of Virginia, the chairman of the Republican National Committee, took the unusual step of arranging a conference call with reporters today to counter publicity about polls showing that Mr. Bush's approval rating is around 50%. The call, which

included Matthew Dowd, a Republican Party pollster who was the Bush campaign's polling director, underscored the apprehension at the White House and in party circles about the president's popularity. In the past, party officials insisted they did not care much about poll numbers. Today, the party officials glossed over Mr. Bush's recent setbacks in the polls and said people should focus on the fact that over time the president's approval rating had been in the range of 50%. 'The consistency of the polling is coming through loud and clear,' Mr. Gilmore said. 'The president has been shown to be consistently in the mid-50's.' But a *Wall Street Journal*/NBC News poll published today put Mr. Bush's approval rating at 50%, the lowest presidential approval rating in five years. Another survey released today, by Reuters and Zogby, showed Mr. Bush was popular with 51% of those polled. The decline was also apparent in the *New York Times*/CBS News poll, published 21st June, which found that Mr. Bush's job approval rating stood at 53%, down seven points from March.

(*New York Times*, 29th June 2001)

The article shows that horse-race polls can become stories in their own right. But more importantly, it exemplifies the way that horse-race polls can play an important role in providing a context for political coverage. Not only do these polls oblige politicians to respond, they set the tone for the way political parties are covered: hence the Bush White House is described as 'apprehensive' after 'recent setbacks in the polls'. This use of polls thus opens the door for a more critical evaluation of President Bush.

This works both ways, of course, and the huge boost received by President Bush after the attacks on September 11th made criticism of his political agenda more difficult. As David Altheide (2004) suggests, these poll numbers were inflected by notions of patriotism. The president's high poll numbers were read as a patriotic response, such that criticism of the president came to be seen as unpatriotic. As CBS News anchor Dan Rather explained, the 'fear' of being accused of 'lack of patriotism' clearly acted as a constraint:

> it is that fear that keeps journalists from asking the toughest of tough questions . . . one finds oneself saying: 'I know the right question, but you know what? This is not exactly the right time to ask it.'
>
> (quoted in Altheide, 2004: 302).

This attitude worked to deflect any controversy from the decision to proceed with tax cuts in the autumn of 2001 (whose prime beneficiaries were the wealthy) *and* to increase defence spending – hence putting the budget in deficit.

Thus when NBC News did a piece on the Bush agenda in October 2001, the plans for funding tax cuts through deficit spending were glossed over because 'George Bush has an exceptionally high level of support':

> *Tom Brokaw*: As any political and military leader knows, if you go to war make sure you have the folks at home solidly behind you, and tonight George Bush has an exceptionally high level of support. I'm joined now by NBC's Washington bureau chief and moderator of *Meet the Press*, Tim Russert . . . Tim, where do we go from here in terms of the American people and what they're going to do about economic stimulus programs and other areas like that?
>
> *Tim Russert*: Tom, the administration and the Democrats have all agreed that the deficit is no longer a major obstacle. If it means deficit spending they're going to spend it. The Social Security lock box has been pried wide open. There is no longer a debate; it is no long an item of discussion.
>
> (NBC News, 8th October 2001)

Not only are the controversial tax cuts now described very much in President Bush's terms (as 'economic stimulus programs'), the support for Bush and the 'war on terror' shifts the context from an 'apprehensive' White House to one no longer subject to scrutiny. This is, of course, facilitated by a degree of capitulation from the political opposition (the Democrats) – another consequence of their perceived weakness in the context of the polls (see Maxwell, 2002, for a further discussion of this issue).

In fact, more specific polls suggest fairly clearly that most Americans *do not* support the use of budget deficits to pay for tax cuts, but we found *no* polls cited in our sample to support this point. Such polls – which run against Bush's policy – *can be deemed irrelevant by the dominant narrative*, which is framed by the horse-race polls showing support for Bush.

So while journalists are, in some ways, responding to a democratic instinct – using public opinion polls to shape political coverage – we also need to be aware that this can work to *suppress* more meaningful coverage of polls dealing with specific, concrete policy issues. In other words, horse-race polls trump issue polls almost every time.

If we develop this analysis to look in more detail at the subjects covered by polls, we can see that less than half the polls used in our press sample deal with specific sociopolitical issues (Table 4.5). This is not due, as some might expect, to an abundance of polls about lifestyle or entertainment, but because of the way polls about government in general (of which horse-race polls are a prominent example) dominate coverage. What links these polls about government in general is that they tend *not* to be policy related, and take the more opaque forms form of approval, disapproval and blame, as we shall illustrate shortly.

While we should not make too much of the TV sample, given its size, it is indicative of the way the news agenda drives the coverage of polls. Hence there were a number of polls on US network news about newsworthy issues such as

Table 4.5 The general topics covered by polls on television and in the press

	US TV (n = 104)	UK TV (n = 28)	US press (n = 804)	UK press (n = 582)
Politicians and government	26%	21%	50%	47%
Economy/business/consumers	10%	21%	7%	8%
September 11th scares and fears	26%	0%	4%	1%
Afghanistan/terrorism	26%	11%	3%	7%
Public services	1%	21%	7%	9%
Crime	2%	4%	6%	3%
Other sociopolitical issues	10%	7%	11%	13%
Other international issues	0%	4%	6%	5%
Sport/entertainment/lifestyle	1%	4%	1%	5%
Other	0%	7%	3%	3%

September 11th, terrorism and the war in Afghanistan, and about Afghanistan and public services (notably the National Health Service) on British television. Polls about other issues (apart from the economy and consumer confidence), however, were few and far between.

We see a greater range of issues covered in our press sample. This included surveys about entertainment or lifestyle issues, such as this in *The Times*:

> according to the findings of a survey undertaken by the mobile phone retailer the PocketPhone Shop, mobile phones are taking on an increasingly important role in all our lives, despite any potential radiation risks. When asked which item they would wish to take with them to a party, 72% of respondents in the 16-to-over-50 age bracket ranked a mobile phone higher than money, handbag/wallet or keys.
>
> (*The Times*, 25th July 2001)

While these lifestyle surveys are not uncommon, their news value is limited: in this example it is linked to a story about the radiation risk of mobile phones. Table 4.5 shows that most issue polls, in both television news and the press, are about more overtly sociopolitical subjects.

We get a more detailed sense of the topics covered by reported polls in Table 4.6. As we can see, a number of polls in the press come under the heading of 'politician's performance'.

This refers not only to approval polls, but to other broad evaluations of politicians, as in the following example from the *New York Times*:

> As of now, though, 4 out of 10 registered voters say they were not paying much attention to the contest. Nearly 60% of Democrats said

the Democratic candidates were 'all pretty much alike,' a point that even some of the candidates have made. More than half of the respondents said they did not know enough about the candidates to say, or were undecided, whether they held a favorable or unfavorable view of them. That said, none of the candidates posted the kind of high unfavorable rating that would signal trouble. While voters' impressions of the candidates remain unformed, a few perceptions are taking shape. Although Mr. Green has tried to portray himself as politically moderate, he is clearly viewed as the most liberal of the Democrats. Four of 10 registered voters described his views as liberal. (Not necessarily a bad thing in a Democratic primary in New York.) By contrast, just 18% of respondents said the same thing about Mr. Vallone.

(*New York Times*, 15th August 2001)

As this example suggests, most of the polls about politicians and government tell us little about what the public think about an issue, so while 46% of polls in the *New York Times* and 41% of polls in *The Times* are vague or general responses to politicians – such as approval ratings and horse-race polls – only 4% and 6% (respectively) concern support or opposition to a government *policy or decision*, as the two following examples do.

We're going to go to the war campaign in a moment. But first, the public mood. A new ABC News/*Washington Post* poll finds today that there is rising doubt in the country about the government's ability to prevent another terrorist attack. Fifty-six percent of people say the US is doing all it reasonably can, but that is down from 68% a month ago.

(ABC News, 7th November 2001)

Privately, some Democrats admit, hammering Bush on the economy is tricky. When a recent poll asked who bore some or a great deal of the blame for the recession, more voters blamed September 11th and Congress than Bush.

(NBC News, 4th January 2002)

But even in these more specific responses, the active agents are still the political classes. In the first example, people are not asked which policy they support, they simply rate the government's ability to deal with something. The second example is in a similar vein: it does not ask what kinds of economic policy people favour, simply the degree to which they hold the president culpable for economic problems. What this does, in effect, is to take the politics out of politics, and reduce the politician to a *managerial* role. All we can assess, in

Table 4.6   The specific topics covered by polls on television and in the press

	US TV (n = 104)	UK TV (n = 28)	US press (n = 804)	UK press (n = 582)
Politician's performance	15%	7%	16%	27%
Elections	9%	14%	30%	14%
Other government policy/ decision	2%	0%	4%	6%
Economy	4%	7%	3%	5%
Business	1%	0%	0%	0%
Employment	0%	0%	3%	7%
Consumption/shopping	5%	14%	4%	3%
Mood after September 11th	5%	0%	2%	0%
Anthrax scare	13%	0%	0%	0%
Air travel safety	9%	0%	1%	0%
War in Afghanistan	14%	7%	2%	6%
Terrorism/terrorists	12%	4%	1%	1%
Health	1%	21%	3%	4%
Education	0%	0%	4%	3%
Railways	0%	0%	0%	2%
Environment	0%	0%	3%	0%
Crime	2%	4%	6%	3%
Racism/segregation	1%	0%	1%	0%
Civil liberties	1%	0%	1%	0%
Gay rights	0%	0%	1%	1%
Royal family	0%	4%	0%	1%
Other domestic issues	7%	0%	4%	4%
Israel/Palestine	0%	0%	2%	0%
Attitudes towards US	0%	0%	3%	0%
Europe	0%	4%	1%	4%
Northern Ireland	0%	4%	0%	0%
Sport/entertainment	1%	4%	1%	5%
Lifestyle, other	0%	7%	3%	3%

this context, is their *performance* – in short, are they good managers or bad managers?

This tells us a great deal about the coverage of politics, and conforms to the pattern revealed by a number of other studies in which politics is seen as being about personality and process rather than policy. So, for example, Janine Jackson's study of the press coverage of the 1992 US Democratic Primary found that only 2% of articles contained any serious discussion of policy issues (Jackson, 1996). Deacon, Golding and Billig (2001) reported a similar emphasis on process and personality in their analysis of the 2001 general election. This is not to say that a politician's 'personality' is irrelevant (even if our ability to judge something like 'personality' through the fog of sophisticated political public relations is questionable). But what matters to most people, most of the time, will be the policy decisions they take.

Moreover, behind this emphasis on political personality and management is a spectacularly glib – but deeply entrenched – diminishment of democratic politics and public opinion. Let us be clear: at the heart of politics are a set of conflicting interests. Do we spend more on education or the military? Do we prize free enterprise above regulations to protect the environment? Should rich people pay a higher proportion of tax than poor people? This is not to say that people will always see the world in terms of narrow self-interest – a wealthy person might value greater economic and social equality above personal financial gain – but in each case, politics is about prioritising one set of interests, such as individual freedom or a healthy environment, against another. Or, to put it another way, politics is about ideology rather than competence. And yet the use of polls in political coverage would seem to suggest the opposite.

Politics and engagement

In the last chapter, we looked at the way in which public opinion in general is more likely to be portrayed as on the right rather than on the left, reflected in an imagined 'middle America' or 'middle England'. This is, we found, particularly the case with the less systematic journalistic references to public opinion, which tend to replicate clichés about 'middle America' or 'middle England'. The representation of polls appears to be more equally balanced in terms of left- and right-wing opinions. The exception here appears to be US television, in which the polls used do suggest a right-leaning public (see Table 4.7, which shows that the coverage of conservative opinions outweighs progressive opinions by nearly four to one), as in the following exchange between Tom Brokaw and Tim Russert on NBC News, in which it is suggested that public opinion is 'more hawkish than many people in official Washington':

> *Tom Brokaw*: Tim, not only are the people of this country behind the President, they're prepared for the long haul.
> *Tim Russert*: Tom, they sure are. Overwhelming support for George W. Bush, and they're perhaps more patient or more hawkish than many people in official Washington. They understand very clearly how difficult this task is ahead, and they seem to be willing to see it through . . .
> *Tom Brokaw*: And, Tim, the remarkable thing to me in this poll, at least, is not just the high numbers that are behind the President,

the fact is that they're prepared to have this war last for as long as three years if necessary.

Tim Russert: Tom, absolutely. The numbers are staggering on that account. And even when we ask people, 'Are you willing to accept casualties?' 78% said yes, 'We understand that is part of this arrangement, part of the deal. We are going to have to pay a higher price including American lives in order to root out terrorism around the world.'

(NBC News, 8th October 2001)

As we suggested in Chapter 3, this image of a 'hawkish' or conservative public only conforms to a very selective reading of the polling data. A more sober analysis of the survey data on US foreign policy suggests that the American public is, on the whole, more multilateral and *less* hawkish than the Bush administration (Kull, 2004). While the US television sample is fairly small, other studies have found a similar pattern of favouring a more conservative picture of public opinion (Lewis, 2001).

Table 4.7   The political leanings suggested by public opinion polls covered on television and in the press

	Left wing	Right wing	Mixed	Unclear	Total
US press (n = 804)	15.8%	12.6%	4.1%	67.5%	100%
British press (n = 582)	9.1%	12.0%	3.6%	75.3%	100%
US television (n = 104)	7.7%	29.8%	0.0%	62.5%	100%
British television (n = 28)	14.3%	14.3%	0.0%	71.4%	100%

In Chapter 3, we also discussed what appeared to be a strong preference for apolitical opinions in the news media. Politically identifiable opinions, we found, are *most* likely to emerge in the coverage of demonstrations and polls. Nevertheless, this is only a matter of degree, and Table 4.7 shows that *most* of the opinions represented in polls are difficult to classify in ideological terms, as the following examples illustrate:

An ABC News poll shows that Americans, who spent $930 each on Christmas two years ago plan to spend just $775 this year. Some industry analysts are forecasting that this could be the worst shopping season in more than a generation.

(ABC News, 21th November 2001)

According to an ABC News poll, 77% of Americans say they are concerned about anthrax, but not scared. And a whopping 92% believe their mail is safe. . . . The polls show that those living in the East are more likely to express fear about their mail.

(ABC News, 25th October 2001)

Let's take another look at the public mood. How much fear is there in the country? Less we believe than the media sometimes suggests. Our polling, which plays a valuable role understanding public opinion, has interesting data today. Given the anthrax scares, four in 10 Americans, 40% that is, are being cautious when they open their mail. But 60% are not. Thirty-five percent of those we asked are actively seeking information about what to do in the case of a biological attack. But 65% are not. Five percent have spoken to a doctor about anthrax, and 2% have bought antibiotics in case. This represents several million people, and 2% is enough to start a run on a drug. But at least 96% of the public is not buying antibiotics. So is there concern out there? Yes, there is. But no real fear.

(ABC News, 22nd October 2001)

As US taxpayers wait for their W-2 forms to arrive, a new survey indicates the number of Americans who say people should never cheat on their taxes is falling from 87% three years ago to only 76% now. Five percent of those surveyed said taxpayers should cheat as much as possible.

(CBS News, 18th January 2002)

There are shoppers around but the latest survey suggests that people are holding on to their money.

(ITV News, 1st November 2001)

Beate Uhse was a household name in Germany, the most successful of all postwar German businesswomen, and in a showily controversial field. She started out as a pioneer of sex advice and birth-control information in the late 1940s, when most Germans were still ill-informed on such matters. She won grateful admirers, who felt she was doing a public service. Then in the 1960s, rather less idealistically, she turned to building up an empire of pornographic movie houses and supermarket-style sex shops, selling every kind of stimulant, magazine and (later) video . . . Surveys and opinion polls generally found her to be much the best-known of all German women: some 98% of Germans knew exactly who she was.

(*The Times*, 19th July 2001)

> Our new CBS News poll found the sagging economy is still the number one concern of Americans, beating out the war on terrorism.
>
> (CBS News, 7th January 2002)

All of these examples illustrate a point made in the previous chapter: that the news media tend to represent citizens as passive – sometimes responding to politicians, occasionally offering or supporting proposals, but generally engaged in commentary rather than advocacy. We are described as going shopping (or not), being scared (or not) or showing recognition of someone or something. We may even be shown prioritising issues, while holding back on any discussion of what might be done about those issues.

While these examples are typical of our general findings about the media representation of public opinion, when it comes to polls they are only part of the picture. Many polls will, after all, offer a range of policy positions to choose from, thereby indicating a higher level of engagement with those issues, in which the public is shown advocating one position or another. Table 4.8, based on the press sample, tells us more about the nature of this engagement. While we do see many more examples of specific policy proposals than in the general sample (only 5% of references to public opinion on television involve specific policy proposals), this is much less common than the use of polls to show people responding to politicians. Thus 57% of polls in the *New York Times* and 49% in *The Times* involve responses to politicians, while only 16% and 15% (respectively) contain any specific policy proposals to government.

So, for example, when ITV News covered the crisis of confidence around the MMR vaccine in Britain, they reported that: 'In tonight's poll many said Mr Blair should go public [about whether his son had been given the MMR vaccination]' (ITV News, 4 February 2002). While there were other polls done with clear policy proposals on this issue (suggesting the public favoured the option of having single vaccines), in this example the public are seen not telling Tony Blair what he should do, merely what he should reveal (an issue that became an important part of the British coverage of MMR, as discussed in detail by Lewis and Speers, 2003).

Similarly, when a 2,000-word article appeared in the *New York Times* – a piece devoted entirely to the finding of the newspaper's own poll about New York and the upcoming gubernatorial primaries – of the dozens of findings reported, most were about responses to politicians and only *one* told us anything about where New Yorkers stood on a specific subject.

The following extract, for example, tells us that:

- New Yorkers would prefer the governor to have government rather than business experience;
- they thought the schools were poor;
- they were more worried about education than crime;

Table 4.8   Levels of citizen engagement suggested by the press coverage of polls in the USA (n = 804) and Britain (n = 582)

	US	UK
Proposals to government	16.4%	14.6%
Proposals to corporate world	1.1%	0.0%
Proposals to fellow citizens	0.7%	0.0%
Total citizens making proposals	**18.1%**	**14.6%**
Ranking of party/politician performance on specific issue	0.2%	1.5%
Support of/opposition to party or government policy	5.3%	2.6%
Approval/disapproval of politician's behaviour/actions	9.0%	5.5%
Approval/disapproval of politician's handling of an issue	4.4%	5.2%
Other responses to political events/actions	1.4%	1.2%
Horse race/elections	34.6%	30.1%
Apathy, cynicism or lack of engagement towards politics	2.0%	3.2%
Total citizens responding to politicians	**56.9%**	**49.3%**
Discussing social issue/event, no clear proposal	7.5%	11.0%
Discussing own social group, no clear proposal	0.7%	0.7%
Discussing other social group, no clear proposal	1.7%	0.2%
Appeal to government, no clear proposal	0.2%	1.0%
Appeal to corporate world, no clear proposal	0.0%	0.0%
Appeal to fellow citizens, no clear proposal	0.0%	0.0%
Sense of duty to fellow citizens	0.0%	0.0%
Ranking of concern about an issue	1.5%	0.3%
Emotional response to specific issue/event, no clear proposal	3.1%	0.3%
Vague public mood, no clear proposal	0%	0.2%
Total citizens commenting on issue/event/group without proposals	**14.7%**	**13.7%**
Private individual speaks about personal experience	8.2%	14.8%
Consumer confidence	1.6%	3.4%
Total citizens speaking about experiences or as consumers	**9.8%**	**18.2%**
Citizens speaking about sports, celebrity or entertainment	0.2%	4.1%

- they were concerned about housing;
- some were happy with the schools' chancellor and some were not;
- they were generally happy about the state of the city;
- they approved of the mayor but were unconcerned about his departure.

We are thus given a list of reactions and preferences. But the only issue on which they are described as having a *clear policy preference* was that in opposing the elimination of the Board of Education (and even this would appear to be a technocratic rather than ideological preference).

> The poll also indicated some areas of weakness in Mr. Bloomberg's candidacy. A majority of respondents said they would prefer having someone with experience in government rather than experience in the private sector at the city's helm. Of the two areas listed as concerns among respondents, nearly three-quarters said the school system was in bad shape. In contrast to four years ago, when an equal number of respondents in a Times poll listed schools and crime as the top issues the next mayor needed to deal with, in this poll, voters were twice as likely to list education as crime as their top concern. Nearly 60% of respondents said they considered the cost and availability of housing to be a very serious problem. Two-thirds of respondents said it was a bad idea to eliminate the Board of Education as a way of making the mayor more responsible for the schools. About 4 in 10 said they were pleased with the performance of Harold O. Levy, the schools' chancellor; a third said they disapproved. What was most striking about the poll was the extent to which New Yorkers were, at once, happy about the state of the city, generally approving of Mr. Giuliani, yet not worried about his departure.
>
> (*New York Times*, 15th August 2001)

What the polls provide here is the context in which politicians operate, rather than a clear sense of what those politicians should do. So, for example, they are used to suggest that politicians should 'do something' about education, while, effectively, leaving all options open. This is top-down rather than bottom-up politics, providing a great deal of freedom to politicians to set the policy agenda, while giving citizens, at best, a chance to respond.

The problem with this approach is that it makes it possible for a policy debate between candidates to exclude the popular options, regardless of their viability. Polls are thus less about what James Bryce called the 'the will of the majority of citizens', and more about securing a rather weak form of citizen consent for the political classes (Salmon and Glasser, 1995).

We might conclude by saying that while polls portray more active forms of citizenship than other, less formal references to public opinion, the degree to which citizens are shown expressing opinions *to* politicians is still limited. We shall return to this idea in our concluding chapter. In the chapter that follows, we deal with a form of public representation that our study suggests is a far more prominent form of public representation – the vox pop.

5 The *vox populi*

Out of the mouths of babes and citizens

Introduction

This chapter focuses on what happens when television and newspaper stories allow citizens to speak in their own voices, opening up the mass media to the 'sound of the crowd' (McNair, 2000a). The vox pop – the interview with the man/woman in the street – is widely used in television and newspaper stories.[1] Since ordinary citizens neither make nor shape most news stories, they are, almost by definition, excluded from the cast of characters in newspapers and news programmes. Vox pops are an exception to this rule because they allow regular citizens not just to appear on television screens and in newspaper pages, but also to express opinions in their own words. And while the vox pop vignette may sometimes be intended as a light interlude, it also has a more serious purpose, in that it is the form of news coverage in which citizenship is most clearly expressed and defined.

So far, we have established that public opinion is frequently invoked in news stories, but that most references are apolitical, and citizens have scant opportunity to influence the news agenda. This chapter expands on that argument. We found that vox pop interviews are used widely. As Table 5.1 shows, vox pop interviews are the second most common type of reference in both the USA and the UK, surpassed only by the ubiquitous inferences about public opinion. Vox pops account for 41.3% of references to public opinion in the US sample, and 38.7% in the UK sample.

If anything, the high frequency of vox pop interviews is surprising. It takes considerably more effort on the part of news producers to interview a person in the street than it does to make an inference about public opinion, or to refer to public opinion polls. Also, it takes considerably more time in what is already a tight schedule of news broadcasts. We have already established that citizens have very little place within the conversation among elites that makes the news. Yet here we have overwhelming evidence that citizens *are* being given a chance to comment on the news of the day in their own words. This chapter tries to explain this apparent paradox.

Table 5.1 Types of references to public opinion on television news

Type of reference	US television (n = 2,880)	UK television (n = 1,518)
Inference about public opinion	42.8%	44.4%
Vox pops	41.4%	38.7%
Unspecified inference	9.6%	13.6%
Opinion polls	3.6%	1.8%
Demonstrations	2.6%	1.5%

We argue that although vox pops offer a much more substantive representation of citizens than any other type of reference, they have their own limits.
They depoliticise the public sphere because they place interviewees in positions where they speak from a self-interested, personal perspective, rather than
as rational citizens engaged in political discussion. We demonstrate that there
are only a limited number of subject positions from which to speak in vox
pops. Citizens primarily appear as self-interested members of society and as
fans or commentators on popular culture. This trend is not unique to vox
pops, but a feature of references to public opinion more generally. Nevertheless, vox pops *do* offer a few opportunities for citizens to express political opinions. This is especially true in newspapers, which are less restricted in terms of
time and space than television news programmes.

Vox pops as a form of citizen participation

The use of vox pops is a convention of news reporting, but also a response to
particular historical and political circumstances. As Loviglio (2002) has shown,
broadcast vox pops are by no means a new invention. He demonstrates that
'man in the street' interviews formed an integral part of early broadcasting
practices in the USA where, in the 1930s, radio came of age as a media technol-
ogy that was central to the identity of the American nation. Loviglio examines
the show *Vox Pop*, which sought to locate the 'forgotten man in the street' and
probe his opinion and knowledge on a range of topics. As part of this endeavour,
Vox Pop asked detailed opinion questions on issues including child labour, New
Deal legislation, collective bargaining rights and the trial of the Lindbergh
baby's alleged murderer. Such political questions 'seemed to hail a politically
engaged public, a reflection of the New Deal embrace of the forgotten man in
the street as the central figure in a politics of democratic reform' (Loviglio,
2002: 96).

If early practices of radio broadcasting showed an awareness of the need to
construct a politically engaged public, such concerns have resurfaced in recent

years alongside increasing worries about citizens' disenchantment with conventional forms of politics. This disenchantment has caused citizens not only to turn away from electoral participation, but also from the news media charged with keeping us informed about politics. As Hargreaves and Thomas (2002: 6) summarise the findings of their large-scale study of news consumption in the UK, 'there is much diminished interest in and knowledge of political news'. These authors, however, suggest that while people feel disenchanted with politicians, they are overwhelmingly satisfied with the quality of information obtained from television and newspapers.

Nevertheless, the journalism profession is eager to find new ways of engaging the public, as witnessed in the rise of the 'public journalism' movement in the USA (see Glasser, 1999) and the widespread discussions of the relationship between journalism practices and citizen trust in the UK (see Barnett and Gaber, 2001). Among other things, the use of vox pops is now seen by industry specialists as a way of addressing this perceived 'crisis of public communication' (Blumler and Gurevitch, 1995). Richard Tait, former head of news for ITN, sees vox pops as a response to the elitism of news programmes (Richard Tait, personal conversation, 9th November 2004). Their wide use reflects news makers' concerns that 'young people are not particularly aware of politics, and not interested in it'. To him, vox pops serve a similar function to audience participation programmes such as television talk shows, allowing for the entry of non-elite, 'regular' people into the public sphere.

New genres and forms of content are seen to empower citizens in a world where their voices have been so frequently been ignored. In general, 'regular people' only rarely appear on the news. As Gans (1980) documented, 'knowns' or elites are four times more likely than 'ordinary people' to appear in news stories. They are much more likely to appear as eyewitnesses to dramatic crimes or as the victims of terrible events beyond their control (Gans, 1980). The absence of citizens as active contributors to the news has been widely documented by scholars since Gans (see Sigal, 1986; Berkowitz, 1987), suggesting that the 'dependence on elite sources stems from the commercial function of news institutions and the demands on journalists to provide a regular flow of news stories' (Comrie, 1999: 44). As Grabe, Zhou and Barnett found in examining the sources used on *Hard Copy* and *60 Minutes*, 'together these two programs promoted the voices of a small group of empowered elites to shape the worldviews of citizens' (1999: 306). Cottle (2000: 434) observes that 'the organization of news is not geared up to the needs of the socially powerless'. He argues that although citizens do appear in the news, their participation is heavily circumscribed, and they are only infrequently allowed to develop their own points of view (Cottle, 2000: 29). However, new programming initiatives are challenging the historical exclusion of the public from active participation in news making. Television talk shows in particular have been widely studied by media scholars, who have suggested that they do indeed provide opportunities for regular people to affect how a range of social issues are discussed. Recent work by McNair, Hibberd and Schlesinger (2003) argues that:

> The movement from elite to mass representation in public participation broadcasting, and from obsequious deference to rigorous adversarialism in the interrogatory style of programs, has contributed substantially to the development of a distinctively British culture of mediated public access to political debate.
>
> (McNair, Hibberd and Schlesinger, 2003: 109)

On the basis of a production study of several British audience participation programmes, such as *Question Time* and *Jonathan Dimbleby*, these scholars suggest that 'programme makers are generally sincere in their efforts to represent the public, interrogate the powerful, and engage the audience'. Similarly, Livingstone and Lunt's now classic study, *Talk on Television*, demonstrated that talk shows carve out a space for an 'attempt to confront established power with the lived experience of ordinary people' (Livingstone and Lunt, 1994: 160). Television talk shows subvert mainstream culture's reliance on expert knowledge. In the context of these shows, the personal stories of ordinary individuals and their victories and problems told in an everyday language are considered more authentic, legitimate and valuable than the abstracted discourse of experts. Or, as one former journalist put it, 'average citizens sometimes have insights the experts lack' (Seldner, 1994: 89). In the world of television talk shows, expert testimony is rejected because it is seen as 'unreal', cold, disembodied and distant. As talk show host Robert Kilroy-Silk explained it:

> People can be very articulate about things that affect them. Now we do shows with no experts at all – I don't like them. If we're covering cot death I want to talk to women who've experienced it. The best parts of Kilroy are when real people talk to each other. You don't see that anywhere else on TV.
>
> (cited in Livingstone and Lunt, 1994: 98)

These sentiments are echoed in programme makers' views of vox pop interviews. As Richard Tait put it, news editors and producers view vox pops as 'an important antidote to a world where everything is mediated through authoritative voices'. This reflects the 'sense that in an age of spin, vox pops are a way of using language in a more accessible way, in terms which make more of a connection'. The increasing use of vox pops as a 'production value' is integral to news organisations' effort at 'trying to make news more relevant' and expressing issues 'in terms and through metaphors, images and experiences with which the audience can relate' (Richard Tait, personal conversation).

The rise of participatory programming can be seen as indicative of larger shifts in the priorities of news organisations. Jay Blumler (2001) has argued that recent years have seen a transformation of the forms of political communication in a more populist direction. In the past, he suggests that:

> . . . except for occasional vox pop clips, [ordinary members of the public] were mainly represented in the communication process by surrogates, such as opinion poll results and questions put by interviewers to politicians on their behalf. Of course evidence of broad support mattered to all concerned, but on most questions this was presumed to emerge from a 'bystander' public rather than an active citizenry.
>
> (Blumler, 2001: 204)

Nowadays, in what he calls the 'third age of political communication', news organisations have redoubled their efforts to make news palatable to an increasingly impatient audience. He argues that more 'efforts are also made to engage voters in stories by featuring the comments of ordinary citizens. The voiced opinions of men and women in the street are being tapped more often in a veritable explosion of populist formats and approaches' (Blumler, 2001: 205). Among other genres, Blumler mentions talk shows, phone-ins, studio panels, on-air deliberative polling and televised 'people's parliaments'.

These developments can be seen as evidence that news is becoming more consumer-oriented (see Hargreaves and Ferguson, 2000). But they also demonstrate a growing awareness of the need to include the public in substantive ways. However, based on our evidence it appears that even if the 'third age of political communication', marked by a greater attention to the voices of ordinary people, has come to prevail in news media, that orientation has not radically transformed the top-down nature of television news programmes and newspaper stories. Vox pops nevertheless remain ubiquitous because they serve a useful dual purpose in the news programme: they allow for citizen participation, and provide a sense of public opinion.

On how news stories use vox pops

Vox pops never appear at the beginning of a news story. Citizens therefore do not get the opportunity to be the 'primary definers' who provide the framework through which a news event is interpreted (see Hall *et al.*, 1978). Typically, the topic of the story is first introduced by the anchor, who frames the subject area and provides basic information and a preview of the story. Then the correspondent provides further information, introduces the interviews, and seeks out the voices of the man and woman in the street, as in this sequence taken from ABC News:

> And finally tonight, promises for the new year. This is, for many people, a more reflective New Year's Eve. 2001 was marked by the September attacks as well as by a recession, which cost more than a million mericans – million Americans, I should say, their jobs. There are many people who hope 2002 will be a time of recovery. Their New Year's resolutions reflect that. Here's ABC's Erin Hayes. Erin Hayes reporting:
> As resolutions go, you'll certainly hear some of the old standards out there.
>
> *Unidentified woman 1*: 'Spend less money.'
> *Unidentified woman 2*: 'Try to spend less money.'
> *Unidentified man 1*: 'I'm just going to lose weight.'
>
> But for many, this year is different.
>
> *Unidentified man 2*: 'They're going to be things that involve other people, people who I've taken for granted.'
> *Unidentified woman 3*: 'It's not that I didn't care about those things before, but now I think that all the peripheral things in life have sort of fallen away. I guess they came tumbling down with those towers.'
> (ABC News, 31st December 2001)

This story is focused on giving a sense of public opinion on a particular topic. As such, it is like a feature story about public opinion. It is a 'soft news' or 'human interest' story, rather than 'hard news' which provides audiences with crucial information. This is indicated by the placement of stories that include vox pops in the sequence of news programmes. They hardly ever appear in a lead story – our data show that on both US and British television news, only 2.7% of vox pops stem from the top story.

In lengthier stories, vox pop interviews are interwoven with bits of more factual information, to include both expert and citizen perspectives and to add some colour to the story, as in this NBC report on the introduction of the euro:

> It's taken five years to mint 52 billion euro coins, 15 million bank notes, months to distribute them under heavy guard by truck and by train. At the stroke of midnight, the 3,000-year-old Greek drachma all but dead. Germany today, a mock burial of the Deutschmark. Traditional European bank notes shredded, producing mixed feelings

about the euro. In Italy, the young and old struggling to understand the cost of a cappuccino.

Unidentified man: 'It's like I am going to be a tourist in my country.'

Experts say the euro will boost economic growth by cutting costs of cross-border trade and simplify calculations for American manufacturers in Europe.

(NBC News, 31st December 2001)

In this story, vox pops give a flavour of the realities of life in far-away places. The interviews focus not on political issues, such as how Europeans come down on the arguments for and against the euro, but how they are struggling to calculate the price of a cup of coffee.

However, to suggest that stories including vox pops typically don't focus on 'hard news' is not to argue that vox pops are confined to 'soft news' or non-political topics. On the contrary, our study shows that through vox pops, citizens are given the opportunity to express their opinions on a wide range of topics.

Table 5.2 shows that vox pops do not deal with subjects that are substantially different from the other categories of public opinion references. Interesting differences emerge between the American and British samples. If we focus on the television sample, which is most reliable in terms of comprehensively reflecting the balance of subjects, it appears that American citizens were overwhelmingly consulted on issues around September 11th and the war in Afghanistan, while the British public was much more likely to be given a chance to discuss public services. The most frequent subjects of the vox pops are explicitly political – for instance, the US newspaper sample is heavily weighted towards discussion of elections, politicians and political decisions. Despite the dominance of political topics, sports, entertainment and shopping/consumption also make a decent showing.

If we look at how citizens are represented in terms of their political engagement, it is clear that their appearances are haunted by the flaws of citizen representation more generally. On television news, citizens making proposals account for only 5.8% for the US sample, and 3.4% for the UK sample. The figures are slightly higher for the newspaper sample, at 11.8% for the *New York Times*, and 8.6% for *The Times*.

The most significant single category is that of the private individual speaking about personal experience, making up more than 40% of vox pops in the US television sample. Overall, the citizen engagement statistics show us that members of the public are *reactive* when they speak in vox pops. They may, for example, discuss their feelings about September 11th, but primarily from a perspective informed by their own fears and anxieties. They criticise public services, but only on the basis of their personal experiences and frustrations. They

Table 5.2 Subjects of vox pops on television news and in newspapers[a]

	US TV (n = 1,992)	UK TV (n = 587)	*NY Times* (n = 255)	UK *Times* (n = 35)
Politics and government	1.3%	6.9%	39.7%	11.5%
Economy/business/employment	7.8%	3.8%	5.5%	11.4%
September 11th/scares and fears[b]	33.3%	2.7%	3.9%	0.0%
Afghanistan[c]	10.3%	6.3%	5.5%	22.9%
Terrorism and terrorists[d]	11.3%	2.2%	3.2%	0.0%
Public services[e]	7.7%	22.1%	1.2%	31.4%
Crime	0.7%	6.5%	0.4%	2.9%
Racism/segregation	2.0%	0.3%	2.7%	0.0%
Civil liberties, gay rights, human rights	0.5%	0.5%	0.8%	0.0%
Weather	4.1%	0.5%	0.4%	0.0%
Asylum/migration	0.2%	1.7%	1.2%	0.0%
Israel/Palestine	1.0%	0.9%	2.4%	0.0%
Europe	0.5%	3.9%	2.0%	0.0%
Northern Ireland	0.0%	5.3%	0.0%	2.9%
Sport/entertainment	1.3%	11.8%	3.5%	8.6%
Consumption/shopping	4.8%	5.8%	4.3%	0.0%
Environment	0.0%	0.9%	3.9%	2.9%
Natural disasters or accidents	2.4%	3.8%	0.0%	0.0%
Royals	0.0%	0.7%	0.0%	5.7%
Cloning	0.3%	0.0%	3.5%	0.0%
Other issues	10.5%	13.4%	15.3%	0.0%
Total	100%	100%	100%	100%

a. This table includes all subjects that made up more than 1% of the vox pop sample for either USA or UK in TV or newspapers. Subjects in the category of 'other', which are too small to feature in the table, include animal diseases and welfare, attitudes towards the USA, the conflict in Kashmir, festivals, fishing, charities, royals and past wars.
b. Includes references to the mood after September 11th, anthrax, national security and air travel safety.
c. Includes references to the US attack on Afghanistan, the future of Afghanistan, the Taliban and the humanitarian situation in the country.
d. Includes references to terrorism, terrorists and more specific references to Osama bin Laden.
e. Includes stories on health services, education, railways and pensions/retirement.

speak about their experiences on the trains, in supermarkets, and as voters, but from the perspective of the consumer, rather than the citizen. However, even if this is the general pattern, there are exceptions to the rule. Perhaps more than any other type of reference to public opinion in the news, vox pops carve out a space for active citizens to put across explicitly political views. In the following section, we try to understand the main positions from which citizens speak in vox pops. We suggest that there are varied ways of constructing the public,

Table 5.3 Levels of citizen engagement in the television and press coverage of vox pops

	US TV (n = 1,192)	UK TV (n = 587)	NY Times (n = 255)	UK Times (n = 35)
Proposals to government	2.6%	2.9%	10.6%	8.6%
Proposals to corporate world	0.4%	0.0%	0.0%	0.0%
Proposals to fellow citizens	1.8%	0.5%	1.2%	0.0%
Total citizens making proposals	**4.8%**	**3.4%**	**11.8%**	**8.6%**
Ranking of party/politician performance on specific issue	0.0%	0.0%	0.0%	0.0%
Support of/opposition to party or government policy	3.4%	13.1%	3.9%	8.6%
Approval/disapproval of politician's behaviour/actions	0.9%	2.9%	17.3%	2.9%
Approval/disapproval of politician's handling of an issue	0.0%	0.0%	1.6%	5.7%
Other responses to political events/ actions	0.8%	6.3%	5.5%	5.7%
Horse race/elections	0.1%	0.0%	6.3%	8.6%
Apathy, cynicism or lack of engagement towards politics	0.4%	0.4%	4.7%	2.9%
Total citizens responding to politicians	**5.6%**	**22.7%**	**39.2%**	**34.4%**
Discussing social issue/event, no clear proposal	13.9%	25.2%	7.8%	17.1%
Discussing own social group, no clear proposal	9.9%	3.4%	9.4%	2.9%
Discussing other social group, no clear proposal	7.3%	1.9%	6.3%	2.9%
Appeal to government, no clear proposal	0.1%	0.2%	0.8%	0.0%
Appeal to corporate world, no clear proposal	0.2%	0.0%	0.8%	0.0%
Appeal to fellow citizens, no clear proposal	0.3%	0.2%	0.0%	0.0%
Sense of duty to fellow citizens	1.0%	0.0%	0.0%	0.0%
Ranking of concern about an issue	0.2%	0.0%	0.0%	0.0%
Emotional response to specific issue/event, no clear proposal	11.7%	6.0%	3.5%	0.0%
Vague public mood, no clear proposal	0.6%	0.0%	0.0%	0.0%
Total citizens commenting on issue/event/group without proposals	**44.2%**	**36.9%**	**28.6%**	**22.9%**

	US TV (n = 1,192)	UK TV (n = 587)	*NY Times* (n = 255)	UK *Times* (n = 35)
Private individual speaks about personal experience	42.4%	23.2%	16.5%	31.4%
Consumer confidence	0.6%	1.0%	0.4%	0.0%
Total citizens speaking about experiences or as consumers	**43.0%**	**24.2%**	**16.9%**	**31.4%**
Citizens speaking about sports, celebrity or entertainment	1.6%	12.8%	3.5%	2.9%
Total	**100%**	**100%**	**100%**	**100%**

and that some of them are more empowering than others. We look at how the public appears as self-interested consumers, fans and politically active citizens. These subject positions are by no means equally distributed across the sample. The view of the citizen as self-interested consumer predominates, whereas the occasions when citizens appear as politically active are few and far between.

Citizens as consumers: the self-interested members of society

Stories in which citizens are positioned as self-interested members of society, responding to political news by talking about how it affects their personal lives, are by far the most common type of vox pops identified in our study. The sample is dominated by vox pops in which citizens are given a voice to represent a 'broad swathe of public opinion' (Richard Tait, personal conversation) – but what they are really expressing is a private opinion on the basis of their personal experience as consumers.

The most obvious example of this tendency is the large number of stories about consumption and shopping. Indeed, in our sample as a whole, with the exception of *The Times*, stories about shopping and spending made for one of the largest categories of vox pop topics (6.8% on US TV, 5.8% on UK TV, and 3.9% in the *New York Times*). The vox pop interviewee, then, often makes it into the news as a shopper:

> Patricia Solon, 67, of Kensington, said: 'Coming to sales at Harvey Nichols is never stressful – the other shoppers are very genteel. No one elbows each other out of the way for bargains because people here are

very friendly and very nice. I'm hoping to buy some Italian clothes and I'm meeting friends here to turn it into a day out.'

(*The Times*, 28th December 2001)

The bright decorations and the stores stockpiled with merchandise are facing Americans reluctant to spend. At the Willowbend Mall in Dallas.

Unidentified woman 1: 'We're mostly just out enjoying the Christmas decorations.'

Unidentified man: 'I don't think there is some of the – the sense of euphoria we used to have.'

Unidentified woman 2: 'We've probably looked at our list at little bit more carefully. It's a little shorter this year.'

And a lot shorter for many. An ABC News poll shows that Americans, who spent $930 each on Christmas two years ago, plan to spend just $775 this year. Some industry analysts are forecasting that this could be the worst shopping season in more than a generation.

(ABC News, 21st November 2001)

Consumers do not have to be passive, of course. Some news items do carry references to politically engaged consumers. So, for example, ITV News covered a story about consumer associations lobbying for a change in catering laws (ITV News, 2nd February 2002). Yet references to a politically active group of consumers are rare. With the exception of consumers in America shopping as a patriotic act of defiance against terrorism (discussed in more detail in Chapter 7), consumers are usually shown as having little awareness of their wider social community, of political and economic contexts, or of the consequences of consumerism.

So, for example, rises in petrol prices are generally discussed as an individual consumerist issue – and hence seen as negative – rather than a broader environmental issue, where they may be seen as more beneficial:

Nearly everyone that came through the Amoco station this afternoon said the same thing. Kristen Gruidl put just $7 worth of gas in her Jeep Wrangler because of the high prices. Another man bought $10 worth of gas, about four and a half gallons, enough to get to the airport in his Honda Accord. 'This is crazy,' he said, speeding away.

(*New York Times*, 30th August 2001)

In this kind of news coverage, consumerism trumps citizenship almost every time. What matters to the individual consumer – the price of petrol – is more important than broader community concerns about the environmental (and foreign policy) consequences of dependence on cheap oil.

Even in stories about public services, the pattern of viewing members of the public as consumers, rather than citizens, is replicated. In these stories, individuals are interviewed not to gather information about public opinion on how citizens thought public services could be improved. Instead, the stories provide evidence of patients' personal experiences and feelings about services that they have used, as in the following story about the use of Botox, broadcast on CBS News:

> The CBS Evening News ends tonight with the never-ending search for an easy answer to looking younger. The hot shot solution now being touted is a shot of well-known toxin. But CBS News medical correspondent Elizabeth Kaledin reports there are a few wrinkles to consider. Elizabeh Kaledin reporting:
> Alisa O'Toole was tired of people confusing her frown lines with her feelings.
>
> *Ms Alisa O'Toole (Botox recipient)*: 'People would always think that I was mad, and I'm not angry.'
>
> So she opted for the popular treatment Botox: part poison, part fountain of youth.
>
> *Unidentified woman*: 'Very good. It doesn't hurt at all.'
>
> An injectable drug made from toxins that cause botulism, which paralyzes muscles in the face and makes wrinkles disappear.
>
> *Ms Alisa O'Toole*: 'The change was I could still go like this – hi – but I couldn't do frown.'
>
> (CBS News, 7th February 2002)

This use of vox pops perpetuates a view of citizens as consumers committed to their own pleasure and self-improvement. They speak in individualistic and privatised terms, and appear ignorant and childish in their inability to consider the long-term consequences of actions – in this case, injecting toxins into their faces. The implicit ideological message is that the 'common' person is incapable of rational reflection, only living for the moment.

Another common category of stories that included vox pops focused on the consequences of the downturn in the economy. These stories highlighted how events like the stock market crash and decreases in interest rates have affected the lives of ordinary people, as in this example from ABC News:

And now, the big news about the economy today. The Federal Reserve cut interest rates today for the 10th time this year; a half a point to 2%, which is the lowest level in 40 years. And there was a solid rally on Wall Street. The Dow Jones industrial average was up 150 points to close at 9,591. On the Nasdaq stocks were up 41 points.

The Federal Reserve outlined what Americans already know in delivering its rate cut today. 'Heightened uncertainty and a deterioration in business conditions both here and abroad are damping business conditions. The risks are weighted mainly toward economic weakness.' At a job fair in Atlanta today, out-of-work Americans doubted there was much Alan Greenspan could do for them.

Unidentified man: 'Unless his cut is going to help me get a job, it's probably not going to make any difference to me.'

(ABC News, 6th November 2001)

Here, the vox pops interview is implied to capture the public opinion of 'out-of-work Americans'. However, it is a public opinion that takes an interest in financial policy from the vantage point of the self-interested consumer, rather than from the perspective of someone interested in making the world a better place or, a bit more mundanely, in improving the economy. The interviewee appears to be uninterested in large-scale political events because they don't impact directly on his own life. At the same time, this subject position allows the interviewee to make an explicitly political point. It gives him the opportunity to question the wisdom of cutting the interest rate, if the aim of doing so is to reduce unemployment. When government plans and actions *do* affect the lives of citizens, vox pops are solicited to illustrate the concrete impact of those decisions:

Sitting in her conservatory, Elizabeth Harris says she and her neighbours cannot take the noise any more. 'The planes come every 90 seconds, all day. One goes over, and you can already hear the rumble of the next one. The windows rattle and you can't even speak in the garden,' says Harris, an accountant who has lived in Kew with her husband Jeffery since 1975. Glance at the sky and you see the long queue of jets glinting in the sun as they track down the glide-slope to Heathrow's runway 27R. The worst, says Harris, are the Far East arrivals that start at 4.30am.

Harris is one of the million or so Londoners estimated to be affected by the unceasing din of airliners feeding into Europe's busiest airport. A middle-class campaigner with the ClearSkies anti-noise group, she embodies everything the Government is up against as it gropes for a way out of a seemingly insoluble mess.

(*The Times*, 12th June 2001, feature section)

In these vox pops, citizens express 'common sense' positions and embody a populist political stance. 'Common sense', however, is not necessarily the same as the common good. The people who are consulted for their opinions are constructed as if they act not out of a sense of the better long-term good of society, but are purely in it for their own short-term interests.

In a story on overfishing, resulting in the decision of some restaurants to take certain types of fish off their menus, a fishmonger is consulted for her opinion on this move. She predictably says, 'I think it's an overreaction' (BBC News, 8th February 2002). This is perhaps a popular point of view, but it is not necessarily one that is based on what is best for all. Similarly, in a story on the moves to bring in new managers in failing hospitals, a patient comments, 'I can't really complain . . . I had excellent service' (BBC News, 11th February 2002). Such a representation demonstrates a tendency that Nina Eliasoph (1998) has referred to as 'the evaporation of politics in the public sphere'. It illustrates that when citizens are given a voice in public, they are expected to speak as self-interested, depoliticised consumers, rather than as engaged citizens. This, in turn, means that the public sphere, as the 'sphere of private people come together as a public' to discuss matters of common concern (Habermas, 1989: 27), is effectively devoid of content.

Citizens as commentators on popular culture: critics and fans of sports and celebrities

By contrast to stories about political news, in which citizens are only rarely seen to offer public-minded thoughts, reports on sports and popular culture appear to carve out a space for substantive opinions. Participation in sports could be seen as a 'safe' way of expressing patriotism. Sports fandom is frequently tied to a sense of national and regional identity (see Brookes, 2002; Smith and Porter, 2004). The link between sports fandom and patriotism is often made explicit in news stories, as in the following example from CBS News, from the period immediately following September 11th:

> Prompted by recent events, the NFL's Chicago Bears said today they are turning down multimillion-dollar corporate offers to rename their football stadium. It will remain a tribute to US servicemen and women – Soldier Field. And as John Blackstone reports now, the American spirit is also on display on the baseball field, thanks to a giant named Bonds – Barry Bonds. John Blackstone reporting:
> (. . .)
> Now, for every home run he hits, Bonds is donating $10,000 to relief efforts in New York.

Mr Bonds: 'We're a strong nation here, and we're – we – we don't give up.'

For Americans who had to go without any professional sporting events for almost a week, the national pastime remains part of the nation's fabric.

Mr Bart Quinn (baseball fan): 'All the flags that we see, it brought the country together. I think, we were a little separated for a while.'
(CBS News, 28th September 2001)

In the context of a story about sports, a baseball fan is given an opportunity to speak authoritatively about nationalism – a topic on which he would probably not otherwise have been consulted. At the same time, expressing your citizenship by being a spectator in sporting events is profoundly apolitical.

However, sports is not the only realm in which citizens are given a voice as fans or commentators. They are also consulted for their opinions about celebrities and soap opera stars. For example, an ITV news story included vox pops of the fans of actress Julie Goodyear, who were pleased to have her back on the soap opera *Coronation Street* (ITV News, 30th January 2002). Another ITV story looked at how shoppers in a mall responded to the re-release of a George Harrison single, asking them for their opinion on whether it would top the charts for Christmas (ITV News, 7th December 2001). These examples differ from the vox pops in which citizens respond to political news because they actually invite the interviewees to express substantive opinion and judgments, as experts on sports and popular culture. The public appears to have more authority as consumers of pop culture products and individuals than they do as citizens of a democratic society.

Citizens as politically active

However, this is not to suggest that politically active citizens are entirely absent from the vox pop sample. They may be rare, but they are occasionally allowed into the public sphere, especially in newspaper stories. When citizens offer substantive opinions about politics, it is often in the form of emotional reactions to political events or leaders. Thus, one unidentified man expresses anger over the September 11th terrorist attacks by saying that his 'initial reaction is to just go and nail the bastards' (CBS News, 31st December 2001). In another example, this one from the *New York Times*, a citizen is critical of George W. Bush on the basis of his foreign policy:

'He scares me and I'm uneasy about his approach to foreign policy,' Jim Carabanas, 57, an independent who was a poll respondent, said in a follow-up interview yesterday. Mr Carabanas, a painting contractor from Austintown, Ohio, added, 'It's going to take some time until he gets the experience he needs.'

The story goes on to discuss Mr Bush's approval ratings in terms of his handling of foreign policy and the environment (*New York Times*, 21st June 2001).

In a time of great concern about the excesses of corporate power, vox pop interviews mobilise outrage over the excessive privilege afforded to big business. For instance, a CBS News report highlights the unfairness of corporate tax in this way – the correspondent introduces the problem, but the moral judgment is articulated by a vox pop from 'pro-business Atlanta':

> Yet many of America's marquis corporate names pay no federal taxes. Some even get millions in tax rebates. According to a study by the Citizens for Tax Justice in 1998 from the Fortune 500, 24 corporations reported a total of $12 billion in pre-tax profits. With tax breaks, not only did they avoid the usual 35% tax rate and paid nothing, together they earned another $1.2 billion in tax rebates. That's a difference of $5.5 billion, equal to the total 1998 federal taxes paid by everyone living in these four states. Even in pro-business Atlanta, that disparity hits home.

> *Unidentified man*: 'I think big business ought to pay taxes just like the rest of us do.'
>
> (CBS News, 18th January 2002)

Using the 'ordinary person' with whom the audience can identify is a way of mobilising moral outrage without compromising the objectivity of the reporter. While journalists are generally 'reluctant to take responsibility for the moral judgments embodied in [their] stories' (Ettema and Glasser, 1998: 155), they seek out individuals who can give voice to those moral judgements, and who can put 'a human face on the numbers' (Ettema and Glasser, 1998: 198). In this rare example, the ordinary person calls upon government to change its tax policy. Even if this statement can be understood within the context of journalistic strategies for infusing a moral dimension into their stories, it is also a clear instance of a politically active citizen, placed in a position of expressive authority. This example demonstrates to us that while citizens are rarely seen to have technical or policy-making expertise, they are much more likely to be endowed with moral authority; an authority that comes from common sense rather than formal credentials.

Vox pop interviews rarely allow for open criticism of political leaders and their policies – our data suggest that when this does happen, it is usually with foreign vox pops, who are often given more leeway to express opinions than domestic vox pops. It is as if foreigners are, by default, seen to be authorities on those countries. In the following example taken from NBC News, an Egyptian woman expresses her outrage at US foreign policy:

> *Unidentified woman*: 'If the United States really doesn't want a terrorist attack to happen like that again, it – it had better not start taking actions that aggravate the whole world.'

> Recent polls show 75% of Egyptians oppose the US strikes. Political scientist Mona Makrame says this anger is a reaction to US foreign policy in the region.
> (NBC News, 22nd October 2001)

Another similar example, from the *New York Times*, uses vox pops to take a critical look at the politics of the populist right-wing Austrian politician Jörg Haider:

> 'The biggest problem with Jorg Haider,' the populist right-winger whose party shares power in Austria, 'is that he has two words – "Auslander raus!" ("Foreigners out!"), but we need two hours to answer it,' said Dieter Bogner, a museum designer and one of Vienna's great and good.
>   Mr Haider has never actually used those words to insist that foreigners leave – he is more concerned that more do not arrive. But he 'creates a very unpleasant atmosphere, and it takes a lot of time to fight it,' Mr Bogner said. 'He finds simple, short, understandable sentences to get his point across – if he were talking about peace and brotherhood, he'd be great.'
> (*New York Times*, 7th February 2002, section A: 3)

Here, a citizen of a foreign country gains expressive authority from being described as one of 'Vienna's great and good'. He has no formal credentials that allow him to pass judgment on a political leader, yet he analytically describes the role of Haider in transforming the public debate in Austria. The example shows that foreigners are given the opportunity to express political opinions and analyse events in a way that not only brings audiences closer to the lives of people abroad, but also demonstrates to them that citizens can be active and engaged.

Citizens and the agenda

Vox pops are celebrated by some journalists as the authentic voices of ordinary people, as opposed to the dry and abstract words of the expert. They are also seen as ways of compensating for the lack of diversity in television and newspaper representations. However, the diversity represented by vox pops is not without its limits. Our research on gender in vox pops shows that in UK and US television news, vox pops fall short of equal representation. Of those vox pops where gender could be identified, females made up 43% in the US sample, and 44% in the UK sample.

And even if the faces shown and the voices heard do show a wider cross-section of the population than that provided by politicians, journalists and pundits, there is rarely much new in the ideas they're expressing. This is not due to the lack of originality of citizens, but the lack of ways for them to speak with authority. This chapter has shown that in vox pops citizens are, in the main, allowed to speak from a reactive and self-interested viewpoint, rather than being in a position to offer specific ideas and proposals. As Richard Tait put it, 'people might have a four-part plan for saving the world involving policies which haven't been discussed anywhere else. If you share those with the audience, they will become confused. It's better to get them from someone who actually has a chance to make them happen.' (Richard Tait, personal conversation)

This is not due to an absence of ideas and plans on the part of citizens, but rather because of the perception that they don't have any legitimacy in their attempts to influence policy making. Such a perception is certainly justified in terms of conventional understandings of expertise. The ultimate consequence of this position, however, is that citizens are only allowed to contribute emotional reactions, not reason or knowledge, to the political process. As Bent Flyvbjerg argues, 'power is knowledge. Power determines what counts as knowledge, what kind of interpretation attains authority as the dominant interpretation ... Defining reality by defining rationality is a principal means by which power exerts itself' (Flyvbjerg, 1998: 226–7). What counts as rational and convincing arguments is, in most discursive practices, not determined by debate, but fixed in place on the basis of hegemonic interests (see Gramsci, 1971: 271). In the context of news media, it means that regular people have little opportunity to set the agenda and to express political ideas. What counts as rational, convincing and possible is already defined by politicians and journalists. As Richard Tait concludes:

> In the main, when you are covering news, you're dealing with an agenda as it's defined by political parties, corporations, lobbies; the

establishment. The agenda is created by the activities and languages of those groups. Alternative ways of looking at the world do not get much looking in.

(Richard Tait, personal conversation)

The message is that while ordinary people can bear witness to politics and be the victims of decisions made above their heads, politicians and experts are the only ones who can come up with solutions. As Karpf (1988: 106) has put it, the public is called upon primarily to provide emotional content, supplying the 'raw material which experts process into cause and effect, problem and solution' in news stories.

Conclusion

Vox pops allow citizens to participate in political debates, and react to events as they unfold. They provide a genuine opportunity for mediated public opinion formation. However, with this opportunity comes a series of challenges, as vox pops are haunted by the flaws that plague mass democracies more generally. Contemporary Western societies are characterised by a division of labour whereby politicians and experts make decisions, the media report on them, and citizens merely react to them (see Bohman, 2000). When regular people play little role in making the decisions that shape their lives, they are seen as ill equipped to substantively comment on these decisions. The role of the people who are interviewed in vox pops on television news programmes, is largely one of responding to the doings of politicians and other power holders, rather than shaping the world through their own actions. This leaves us with the impression that they are outsiders to the political process.

In the world constructed by vox pops, there are few real citizens, but a vast mass of consumers who can express approval or disapproval for the policies of government, the decisions of corporations, shifts in the global economy and the whims of the weather. We might hear people complaining about the state of public services and how they have personally been inconvenienced by delays, strikes and cuts in spending. But we are much less likely to see or read vox pops in which people advocate more public spending, less privatisation or any other coherent and explicitly political response to the problem. The citizens who speak in vox pops in television and newspaper stories inhabit a strange realm between the public and the private sphere: the sphere of the consumer. They are openly discussing matters of common concern in their own voices, but they do so in ways that demonstrate an interest for their own welfare, rather than the common good.

Yet this chapter has also suggested that there are opportunities for citizens to actively participate in news through vox pop interviews and that, if anything, the trend in journalism is toward the greater inclusion of audience viewpoints. The representation of citizens on television news is profoundly structured by production conventions and constraints, but it may also be changing to allow citizens to have a greater voice. Citizens are seen as capable of expressing themselves authoritatively on matters that are relevant to their own lives and experiences, and on issues of morality. When they occupy these subject positions, they can condemn the actions of politicians and corporations and mobilise broader public outrage by sharing their emotions. This is important because such inclusion addresses what Barry Richards (2004) has referred to as the 'emotional deficit' in political communication, or our failure to acknowledge the politically activating potential of communicative forms that engage people's feelings. Along those lines, Ted Glasser (1991) proposes that personal story telling in the public sphere can create solidarity between strangers because it can:

> cut through abstractions and other obscurities and focus on the everyday meaning of life and our dealings with it. Stories enable us to think creatively and imaginatively about our experiences and the experiences of others; they empower us to interpret and thereby comprehend the endless details of life . . . [Stories have a] basic role in transforming individual and essentially private experience into a shared and therefore public reality.
>
> (Glasser, 1991: 235–6)

If anything, the wide use of vox pops encourages such story telling and, through it, creates a space for us to understand each other. Such understanding stops short of real political efficacy. But it does contribute to democratising the discourse of news.

These changes toward a greater democratisation of news have come about as a result of a growing awareness among journalists that the public is unhappy with their lack of representation in news stories. The presence of vox pop interviews in news stories has not transformed the top-down nature of the news agenda, but it *has* brought a wider variety of voices, faces and stories to our television screens and newspaper pages. Whether a greater diversity of individuals can transform the public sphere in terms of the kinds of *ideas* being expressed and discussed remains to be seen.

Note

1. The vox pop category focuses on the use of 'ordinary' people in news stories and therefore excludes people interviewed because of their expertise, or people who have merely witnessed an event. In the context of newspapers, our study

6 Talking about the public
Inferences about public opinion

Introduction

This chapter looks at the most common and, at the same time, least substantiated, forms of reference to citizens and public opinion. It examines what happens when journalists, politicians or experts make broad statements about public opinion. The chapter focuses on two categories, which, when taken together, make up the vast majority of all the references to public opinion: those of *inferences about public opinion*, and *inferences about the opinion of unspecified populations*.

First, the category of inferences about public opinion involves statements that *infer* something about public opinion in general, without reference to polling data or other systematic evidence. For instance, in a BBC News story on the downfall of the Taliban in Afghanistan, the correspondent notes that 'the mood among Kabul citizens is one of relief' (BBC News, 15th November 2001). Second, *inferences about the opinion of unspecified populations* are even more vague. They refer to some form of unspecified opinion without providing any systematic evidence, as when the correspondent in a story on a visit by Tony Blair to Washington interjects that 'some people accuse Blair of neglecting the domestic agenda' (BBC News, 7th November 2001). The unspecified inference is the weakest form of reference to public opinion, insofar as it tells us little about the population it represents. Nevertheless, statements such as 'some people say' or 'some observers believe' imply that the universe of those who hold the position is broader than just the one person who is usually interviewed to articulate that position.

We have separated the two types of inferences about public opinion because we believe they work slightly differently. Both are shorthands for complex processes, but inferences about specific formations of public opinion tend to be central to the news story, while the unspecified inferences are much more vague and often appear in stories simply to provide a balance or counterpoint to the dominant point of view.

The chapter shows that inferences about public opinion, regardless of their type, do important narrative and ideological work. Most inferences about public opinion are made by journalists, rather than sources. Such statements rarely appear as the sole references to public opinion in a story, but are usually followed by other types of references, such as vox pop interviews, images of demonstrations, or, in rarer cases, evidence from public opinion polls. They contextualise other forms of information about public opinion, providing an interpretive lens that allows the audience to make sense of the story. But they also do important ideological work. They impose unity, coherence and order to a field of public opinion that is, in reality, much more complex and messy than can be described in a sound bite. And they provide a way of using public opinion to anchor claims made in the news story, without threatening the objectivity of the reporter. References to public opinion can thus be used as 'a strategic tool in the service of instrumental action by individuals and groups associated with the exercise of power' (Beaud and Kaufmann, 2001: 77).

At the same time, we should recognise the politically empowering fact that public opinion is ubiquitous in news stories. It demonstrates a key principle of democratic theory, which is that the exercise of power has to be seen as legitimate in a democratic society, and to gain such legitimacy, decisions must be made in line with public opinion, based on the consent of the governed (Peters, 1995: 3). The mass media's attempts at representing public opinion show that they are paying heed to this requirement for political legitimacy. However, whether their representations of public opinion bear any relationship to ideals of citizen participation in politics is more questionable.

How are inferences made?

If we look at the distribution of inferences about public opinion – specified *and* unspecified – in our television sample, it becomes apparent that this is a central form of reference to public opinion. In the US sample, inferences about public opinion of both types make up a total of 53.5% of all references to public opinion, while in the British sample, they account for 57.9%.

Because our television sample is based on a comprehensive content analysis of all news stories during the period of the study, whereas the newspaper sample is based on a keyword search, the television data are more reliable in terms of identifying the distribution of types of reference to public opinion. The press sample, on the other hand, is skewed towards public opinion polls, because 'poll' was one of our search terms. Nevertheless, the two types of inferences about public opinion make up a total of 37% of all references in the *New York Times* and 36% in *The Times*.

The sheer quantity of inferences makes sense. They are by far the most casual form of reference to public opinion, and they also serve to summarise

Table 6.1 Types of reference to public opinion on television news

Type of reference	US television (n = 2,880)	UK television (n = 1,518)
Inferences about public opinion	42.8%	44.4%
Vox pops	41.4%	38.7%
Unspecified inference	9.6%	13.6%
Opinion polls	3.6%	1.8%
Demonstrations	2.6%	1.5%

Table 6.2 Types of reference to public opinion in newspapers[a]

Type of reference	New York Times (n = 1,679)	The Times (n = 1,023)
Opinion polls	47.4%	56.9%
Vox pops	15.0%	3.4%
Demonstrations	0.2%	1.9%
Inference about public opinion	28.1%	27.0%
Unspecified inference	8.7%	9.4%
Letters	0.5%	1.5%

a. Chi-square tests suggested that most of the US/UK differences were statistically significant (p <0.05).

complex debates. When the average television news story is at most two to three minutes and the average sound bite seven seconds in length (Berger, 2001: 664; see also Barnhurst and Mutz, 1997), it is unrealistic for journalists to provide an adequate and scientific depiction of public opinion on every story. What they *can* do, however, is to give audiences a sense of prevailing positions on the topic, providing a sounding board for their own opinions. In whichever form they appear, inferences make the public seem like an active participant in the debate (see Fowler, 1991: 73). This goes to the heart of the paradox that this book deals with. That is, journalism moves towards fulfilling its democratic role whenever it endeavours to represent public opinion. At the same time, when citizens and their opinions are represented in the news, that representation is profoundly constructed. As Peters (1995: 16) has put it, public opinion 'claims to be public . . . as an expression of the popular will, but it is often in fact public as a visible fiction before the eyes of the people'.

Inferences are central to the process of constructing the public as a 'visible fiction'. They provide definitive and unitary depictions of public opinion, whether of the population as a whole, or of particular groups. However, this is not to imply that inferences about public opinion usually stand alone in news stories. Inferences are rarely the *only* information given about public opinion in any story, and thus cannot be viewed in isolation from other types of reference. In almost all of the stories that contained references to public opinion – the figures vary between 98% and 100% depending on medium and type of reference – that reference was not the only one in the story, but was accompanied by others providing evidence for the claim made about public opinion, even if that evidence was rarely scientific or systematic. An analysis of ABC News over fifty-eight days of our sample period showed that during this period, forty-two of the final stories of each programme contained one or more inferences about public opinion, but that only six of these stories also included public opinion polls. That is to say, 86% of all inferences about public opinion were not followed up with evidence in the form of polling data.

One example, from ABC News, highlights how inferences construct a 'visible fiction' of public opinion. The story looks at the incidence of anti-Muslim hate crime after September 11th, and tries to assess how US Muslims feel about their treatment:

> . . . Here's ABC's Dan Harris. Dan Harris reporting:
>> Mohammed al-Heidous, a graduate student at American University in Washington, DC, is so scared he's heading home to the Middle East.
>
> *Mr Mohammed al-Heidous*: 'I feel now we are unwelcome here in this country.'
> *Harris*: The fear in the Muslim community is widespread. Tony Zorhavandi, a US businessman of Iranian descent, says he was banned from a commercial flight because he apparently made the pilot nervous. There have been 11 similar reports.
> *Mr Tony Zorhavandi*: 'I was hurt because, like I say, I'm a citizen of the United States of America. And I believe – during the pledge of allegiance, you say "liberty and justice for all". And I feel like, on that day, it wasn't liberty and justice for me.'
> *Unidentified man*: (Foreign language spoken)
>
> Many Muslims also say the FBI is targeting them indiscriminately and inappropriately. Ali Erikenolnu, an American-born electrician, says agents came to his home in New Jersey last week and, in tough questioning, made false accusations and challenged his patriotism.
>
> *Mr Ali Erikenolnu*: 'I always thought they were the good guys. And when they came into my home and acted in the manner that they did, I felt raped.'

While many Muslims complain of harassment and discrimination, they do acknowledge a significant countertrend, a wave of goodwill gestures. Non-Muslims forming protective prayer circles around mosques, wearing head scarves in a show of solidarity and writing letters of support.

Unidentified woman: 'It breaks my heart to see people being attacked and harassed. What happened to the love?'

While these acts of kindness don't get as much attention, Muslims say, even in this time of tension, they've found that decency, not bigotry, is the norm. Dan Harris, ABC News, New York.

(ABC News, 26th September 2001)

This story is centrally *about* public opinion among Muslims. To have any significance and credibility, it relies on being able to make definitive statements, or construct a believable corporate fiction of public opinion. The story provides a reassuring representation of US Muslim public opinion as one that is unified in the belief that American culture is 'decent' rather than 'bigoted'. However, neither this final summary statement, nor the introductory statement which conveys the impression that Muslims 'acknowledge . . . a wave of goodwill gestures', is supported by any evidence – all three vox pop interviews bear witness to the difficulties experiences by US Muslims. The positive sentiments inferred by the voice-over and the correspondent, then, seem to serve a story-telling and ideological role of advancing national unity. This, in turn, puts across a message of common purpose, implying the existence of a more general American public opinion that is tolerant, peaceful and unified.

The example demonstrates that inferences play the role of contextualising claims made about public opinion, but also run the risk of overstating these claims. Some of the ways in which these claims are linked to evidence inhere in the structure of the English language. Along those lines, Fairclough (1995: 122) has suggested that the language of news often makes use of the 'implicit relation' between two proximate sentences. This means that if a statement is made about public opinion in one sentence, it is assumed that the statement is explained or justified by one or more of the sentences that follow. That is, indeed, one of the most common patterns of inferences about public opinion. The following story, which is taken from NBC News and deals with a security scare in Miami International Airport following the discovery of a bullet on the floor, perfectly illustrates the most common structure of a news story that draws on inferences about public opinion. It shows that the inference serves to frame and introduce other references to public opinion – in this case vox pops – and to make them seem representative:

Search dogs sniffed the area, but officials say nothing else was found.

Still, for many passengers, already nervous about flying these days, this pushed them even closer to the edge.

Unidentified man: 'A little bit nervous. I'm travelling with my family, and I was a little bit nervous last night thinking about flying.'

Federal aviation officials have ordered all of the nation's airports and carriers to tighten security in the wake of Saturday's incident over the Atlantic.

Mr Jorge Fernandez (Miami Dade Police): 'You leave your bag and you walk away. I'll sniff it, and I'll snatch it up, and you've got to go find it.'

More National Guardsmen patrolled the terminal inside and out – a sight the Berec family, heading to the Bahamas for Christmas, weren't prepared for but accepted.

Ms Sharon Berec (airplane passenger): 'I was surprised to see the soldiers with the guns. They were surprised.'

(NBC News, 24th December 2001)

Two 'ordinary people' are interviewed for this story. In the first instance, the interview segment is introduced by the correspondent as representative of the opinions of 'many passengers', and the 'implicit relation' to the following sentence likewise suggests that the 'unidentified man' captures the view of 'many passengers'. In the second instance, the correspondent introduces the interviewee as a member of the 'Berec family' – a much more specific type of reference which doesn't imply that Mrs Berec stands in for a broader public opinion. The structure of implying a general public opinion for an initial interview segment and then following it up by a more specific reference is fairly common, and can be found in a slew of stories on topics ranging from cloning (NBC News, 26 November 2001) to plane crashes (ITV News, 12th November 2001) and bioterrorism (NBC News, 17th December 2001).

In some cases, the use of inferences is merely the starting point for a range of different types of references to public opinion. For instance, in an ITV story on the government's decision to reject a proposed ban on smacking, the correspondent introduces a segment on the public opinion surrounding the decision by saying that 'most parents don't approve of smacking, 77% said they want it banned'. After this, the story cuts to an interview with a mother who discusses her feelings about the ban (ITV News, 11th November 2001). Thus the story draws on inferences, polling data and vox pop interviews, offering a fairly comprehensive and systematic picture of public opinion. The inferences, far from being casually made, serve as the starting point for a much more detailed exploration of public opinion. This example shows coverage of public opinion at its best, insofar as it is evidence-based, and uses both available data and anecdotal illustrations to make its point. It takes public opinion seriously. It requires the journalist to spend time on research, rather than relying on their own 'common sense' understandings of public opinion, but it does provide a more rigorous picture of what people actually think. Although public opinion is not predominantly treated in such a responsible way, there are plenty of other instances in our sample of journalists doing their best to reflect the mood of the citizenry accurately.

Either way, these examples demonstrate that inferences are not generally unsupported and made without evidence, but neither are they universally rigorous and reliable indicators of public opinion. What is most consistent about the role of inferences is that they serve to create a vision of public opinion as unified and comprehensible. When journalists draw on inferences as a shorthand description of public opinion, the public comes to appear as a political actor in its own right. It becomes anthropomorphised, or endowed with human characteristics and emotions, as when an ITV News story talks about a 'jittery American public' in a story about concerns over airport security (ITV News, 12th November 2001), or when an NBC story about the anthrax scare describes 'an anxious public traumatized by cleanup crews in moon suits' (NBC News, 5th November 2001).

Through such devices, the journalists and sources who refer to public opinion are given poetic licence to dream up personalities for the imagined public, to describe 'the public mood'. In an interview with *The Times*, Lord Ashdown, the former leader of the Liberal Democratic Party, dismisses Prime Minister Tony Blair as a 'smarmy git', suggesting that the 'public as a whole does not seem to wholly trust or even like him' (*The Times*, 10th September 2001). By personalising the British public, Lord Ashdown implies that there is general agreement on the smarminess of Tony Blair, and that this feeling will ultimately translate into disapproval of his government.

Through these and similar descriptions, the public comes to life as a force to be reckoned with. As Fowler (1991: 15) has pointed out, personalisation is a favourite tool in journalism, because it allows for the promotion of 'straightforward feelings of identification, empathy or disapproval; to effect a metonymic simplification of complex historical and institutional processes.' In the same way that individual political leaders such as Tony Blair or George W. Bush 'stand for' their parties or exemplify larger political processes, so 'the public' or 'the people' stand for the diversity of public opinion. In translating evidence on aggregate public opinion into an inference about a unified, personalised public, the citizenry is mobilised to provide support or dissent in relation to government policies. An ABC story about the war on terrorism thus implies a desire on the part of the public for military action: 'The public has told our polling unit by 2–1, they approve of a war against terrorism, and overwhelmingly the public believes that inaction is the greater peril' (ABC News, 21st September 2001).

In this context, there is one major difference between the inferences to public opinion and the unspecified inferences. While the inferences *always* refer to public opinion, the unspecified inferences are more diverse. In many cases, they provide a different way of referring to public opinion, as when the Rangers footballer Arthur Numan discusses his fears of playing in the conflict-ridden southern Russian city of Dagestan by saying that 'people think nothing can happen to us . . . but that is not true' (*The Times*, 10th September 2001).

Frequently, however, unspecified inferences are used to indicate the presence of opposing points of view, even if it can be unclear whether these perspectives come out of public deliberation or the technical knowledge of experts. For instance, in an ITV story on airport security in the USA, a correspondent introduces an interview with 'some say the system must be overhauled'. This statement is then followed by an interview with a security expert (ITV News, 6th November 2001). Similarly, in an ABC story on the military tactics of the Taliban during the war in Afghanistan, an unspecified inference is used to introduce the opinion of an interview with a UN official:

> Some observers believe the Taliban is shifting its resources to be sure it can protect the areas that matter most.
>
> *(Voice-over)*: In unusually blunt language today, a senior UN official in Pakistan said the Taliban is losing the support of its own people and called for a change.
>
> Mr Frances Vendrell *(UN Assistant Secretary-General)*: 'The vast majority of Afghans have been helpless hostages in their own country for far too long.'
>
> (ABC News, 27th September 2001)

These two examples show that, more than anything, the unspecified inferences are a journalistic device that is an integral part of the 'strategic ritual' of objectivity (Tuchman, 1972). They are practices that 'protect the professional from mistakes and from his critics' (Tuchman, 1972: 679). As Miller and Riechert point out, journalists 'need the protection offered by appeals to objectivity because they work under intense deadline pressures' (2001: 50). By providing evidence of opposing viewpoints, only linked by brief summary statements, the journalists show that there is more than one side to the story without injecting their own opinion or bias into the writing.

Who makes inferences about public opinion?

Whichever form these inferences take, they cannot be taken at face value but should be examined carefully for the context in which they appear, as well as for their ideological implications. In particular, it is important to look more closely at the question of who speaks for the public.

It is important to take a look at who speaks for the public because the ideological and narrative role of inferences in the news stories depend on who is making the inferences. If 'news represents who are the authorised knowers and what are their authoritative versions of reality' (Ericson, Baranek and Chan, 1989: 3), inferences about public opinion are key to this world-making power of news. As shown in Tables 6.3 and 6.4, and Tables 6.5 and 6.6, the overwhelming majority of inferences are made by anchors, reporters and journalists. In the television sample, inferences about public opinion made by the reporter make up almost 80%. In the press, the figure is slightly lower at 73.3%. It should be noted that this distribution of sources is somewhat similar to those that characterise the universe of references to public opinion overall. For both television and newspaper samples, anchors and reporters are responsible for around 80% of all references to public opinion. For unspecified inferences, there is an interesting variation between the television and newspaper sample: on television, 91.3% of all unspecified inferences are made by the anchor, whereas in the newspapers, the average is much lower, at 59.8%.

This disparity between television and newspapers reflects significant differences in how inferences about public opinion are made by journalists in the two media. In both cases, the journalist is in a position of expressive authority; she has the privilege of encapsulating and giving voice to public opinion. Journalistic conventions allow television correspondents their own voice, and often give them the opportunity to make analytical statements. By contrast, the distinctive voice of the journalist is usually absent from a 'hard news' story in the press. This is because explicit judgements, such as ones about public opinion, would be seen as subjective or biased. Print journalists appear to leave such statements to experts, who are responsible for 26.4% of unspecified inferences in the *New York Times*, and 29.2% of references in *The Times*.

When unspecified inferences about public opinion do occur in print news, it often happens outside conventional hard news sections – in opinion pieces, editorials or news analyses, as well as in sports, features, reviews and fashion sections. Journalism outside the hard news pages allows for the expression of opinion, and therefore gives journalists the opportunity to make judgements and truth claims of their own. Opinion, analysis and review pieces have a didactic tone to them which presumes that the writer is in a position to provide useful information to the audience (van Dijk, 1998: 60). Unspecified

Table 6.3 Sources for inferences about public opinion on television

	Anchor/ reporter	Politician at home	Expert at home	Military at home	Politician in other country	Expert in other country	Military in other country
USA (n = 1,232)	77.3%	5.4%	13.2%	0.2%	1.6%	1.8%	0.4%
UK (n = 674)	82.9%	3.0%	11.1%	0.4%	1.8%	0.6%	0.1%
Overall (n = 1,906)	79.3%	4.6%	12.5%	0.3%	1.7%	1.4%	0.3%

Table 6.4   Sources for inferences about public opinion in the press

	Anchor/ reporter	Politician at home	Expert at home	Politician in other country	Expert in other country
USA (n = 477)	68.3%	11.3%	13.0%	2.5%	4.8%
UK (n = 276)	81.9%	8.7%	8.0%	1.1%	0.4%
Overall (n = 753)	73.3%	10.4%	11.2%	2.0%	3.2%

Table 6.5   Sources for unspecified inferences on television

	Anchor/ reporter	Politician at home	Expert at home	Military at home	Politician in other country	Expert in other country
USA (n = 276)	90.2%	1.1%	5.8%	0.7%	1.1%	1.1%
UK (n = 206)	92.7%	3.4%	3.4%	0.0%	0.5%	0.0%
Overall (n = 482)	91.3%	2.1%	4.8%	0.4%	0.8%	0.6%

Table 6.6   Sources for unspecified inferences in the press

	Anchor/ reporter	Politician at home	Expert at home	Politician in other country	Expert in other country
USA (n = 148)	55.4%	12.2%	26.4%	2.0%	4.1%
UK (n = 96)	66.7%	4.2%	29.2%	0.0%	0.0%
Overall (n = 244)	59.8%	9.0%	27.5%	1.2%	2.5%

inferences about public opinion are perhaps prevalent in such pieces because they can be used as a device for legitimating the positions of the author or advancing an argument. For instance, in this review article from *The Times*, unspecified inferences about public opinion are used to set up an argument about public transportation:

> The problem, of course, is that we already know what that price is; we are just not prepared to do enough about it. Travel is one of the subjects on which humans are prone to Orwellian double-think. People want less traffic and a cleaner environment but at the same time they don't want to give up the convenience of their cars. They want

> reliable, clean and punctual trains but they vote in governments that cut back the rail network and then let their remaining ties with the privatised railways fray through indifference and neglect.
>
> (*The Times*, 21st June 2001)

What is interesting about this example is the way in which the author makes a slew of assumptions about public opinion, without providing any support. Such a use of inferences about public opinion – ones in which no other evidence, but only more claims about public opinion are presented in the same story – is prevalent in opinion writing. As readers, we may be inclined to accept that these assumptions about public opinion are made for the sake of argument, and that the rules of providing evidence for claims are suspended in this type of journalism. Newspaper opinion pieces also draw on unspecified inferences about public opinion as a way of establishing an ideological and moral consensus. In an opinion piece published on 12th September 2001, an American writer sought to explain the shock of the September 11th attacks in the following terms:

> When you grow up in America, you know certain things. You live in the best country in the world. You live in the richest country in the world. And you live in a country whose mainland has never seriously been attacked from the outside. You are invulnerable to such a thing.
>
> (*The Times*, 12th September 2001)

In this piece, the notion that the USA is the 'best' and the 'richest' country in the world is taken to be part of a consensus of public opinion in the USA, and used to explain the American national character to the British audience.

Although journalists are the dominant source of inferences about public opinion, they are not the only ones. The other actors making such statements are experts, politicians and military leaders. Each of these actors has a different claim of authority to represent public opinion, and for each of them, these claims work in distinctive ways. After journalists, experts were the most frequent sources of inferences and unspecified inferences. In the television sample, their statements comprised 13.9% of inferences and 5.4% of unspecified inferences, whereas in the press, they made up 14.4% of inferences and a full 30% of unspecified inferences.

In general, journalists increasingly rely on expert sources (Speers, 2004). Scholars have found that experts are now used to comment on a much wider range of issues than they have done historically: 'Today it is the events of the world, not emerging knowledge of the academy, that create a demand for comments, interpretations, and opinions by specialists' (Albaek, Christiansen and Togeby, 2003: 945). As experts move outside the narrower realm of interpreting scientific findings, their role is increasingly one of making sense of the world in a dispassionate way.

Croteau and Hoynes suggest that expert sources provide expertise, knowledge, insight and prestige to journalists' stories (1994: 67). More than that, the use of expert sources can make a report appear more objective and balanced (Steele, 1995: 801). By drawing on experts, journalists supply their stories with 'credibility and authority' (Steele, 1995: 801). While journalists may gather the facts and form an opinion about them, it is ultimately the role of the experts to interpret and analyse the facts and to make the judgements that the journalists cannot (Steele, 1995: 801).

On the basis of this view of experts, they are often seen as reliable sources of information about the world in general, and public opinion in particular, and are consulted for that reason. For example, an ABC story reported on a letter found in the suitcase of one of the September 11th hijackers. The letter quoted the Qu'ran, telling 'the hijackers to stay strong with prayer'. The story reported on the response of US Attorney-General John Ashcroft, who said that 'the letter is a stark reminder of how these hijackers grossly perverted the Islamic faith to justify their terrorist acts'. It then drew on the expertise of Professor Richard Martin of Emory University, who offered the following assessment of Muslim opinion: 'I know of no Muslim who would say that it – that it is a good use of the Quran. It's – no, it's a bad use of the Quran for – for – for most rational beings' (ABC News, 28th September 2001). The points made by Ashcroft and Martin are similar: both denounce the use of the Quran to urge on the hijackers. However, while Ashcroft offers the 'official' reaction, Martin speaks as an expert, and hence as the voice of objectivity and reason. Unlike Ashcroft, he is constructed as someone who can accurately represent Muslim public opinion.

This is not to say that political figures like Ashcroft are barred from making statements about public opinion. On the contrary, political figures are the third most frequent sources of such claims in our study. The frequency of politicians making inferences about public opinion and unspecified inferences varies greatly across media – while politicians make 6.3% of inferences and 2.9% of unspecified inferences on television, they do so much more prominently in the press, accounting for 12.4% of inferences and 10.2% of unspecified inferences.[1]

When politicians refer to public opinion, they ostensibly do so as 'representatives of the people' (Manning, 2001: 145). In actuality, though, their references to public opinion usually serve an ideological function. They legitimate the politicians' statements, suggesting that they have public support for their actions and claims. However, journalists believe that politicians' claims are suffused with ideological content or 'spin' (see Barnett and Gaber, 2001; Franklin, 2004), and therefore should not be taken at face value. One example of how the news media deal with politicians' references to public opinion is this NBC story which reports on President Bush's controversial anti-terrorism measures:

> *Tom Brokaw (anchor)*: And in Washington tonight, President Bush defended two controversial policies in the anti-terror campaign: the roundup of Arabs and Arab-Americans here at home and the authorization of military tribunals for terrorists who are caught. The president said US officials will act with justice and fairness, which he said is more than the terrorists grant their victims.
>
> *President George W. Bush*: 'Ours is a great land, and we'll always value freedom. We're an open society, but we're at war. The enemies declared war on us, and we must not let foreign enemies use the forms of liberty to destroy liberty itself.'
>
> *Brokaw*: Civil liberties groups and some lawmakers, including prominent Republicans, have questioned whether some of the administration's tactics, especially the closed military courts, could violate due process rights.
>
> (NBC News, 29th November 2001)

Bush's rhetorical deployment of national identity is not left unquestioned. His use of 'ours' and 'we' to justify controversial decisions is juxtaposed to criticisms from what are constructed as legitimate opponents. As Steve Barnett has argued, the dark side of representations of public opinion comes to the fore when powerful actors in the political process use the notion of the public to 'lend a spuriously populist credibility to their own agendas' (Barnett, 2001: 308). However, NBC News here shows an awareness of this danger, drawing attention to the arguments against Bush's policies. This example shows that while experts' inferences about public opinion are often actively solicited by journalists, and used as objective 'facts' in the story, a politician's inferences are much more likely to be viewed with suspicion, as well as countered by critics. By not accepting the claims about public opinion made by politicians, journalists show themselves as watchdogs on government and also demonstrate their allegiance to the ideals of objectivity and balance. Thus, far from being 'stenographers to power' (Hertsgaard in Croteau and Hoynes, 1994: 18), journalists sustain their independence through such 'strategic rituals' of their profession.

Our data and the examples cited here demonstrate that not all inferences about public opinion are created equal. The claims of journalists are ubiquitous and form an integral part of the news narrative, while expert statements are solicited as 'facts', and politicians' rhetorical flourishes are received with deep suspicion.

Whose opinion is inferred?

Either way, journalists, experts and politicians are rarely making inferences about public opinion in universal terms, but usually refer – sometimes explicitly, sometimes implicitly – to a particular population, whether it be the nation as a whole or the public of air passengers, nurses and doctors, or farmers. Tables 6.7 and 6.8 show which populations are the most frequent subjects of opinion inferences.[2]

Table 6.7 Main populations, TV inferences[a]

US TV population (n = 1,232)	% of inferences	UK TV population (n = 674)	% of inferences
Unspecified members of the public/nation	44.7%	Unspecified members of the public/nation	29.5%
People from specific town/area	14.4%	People from specific town/area	17.8%
Consumers/shoppers	7.6%	Consumers/shoppers	6.7%
Muslims/Arab population	4.5%	Sports fans	5.8%
Air passengers	4.5%	Parents	4.7%
Nurses and doctors	2.4%	Nurses and doctors	4.0%

a. This table shows the six most frequent populations referred to in inferences about public opinion.

Table 6.8 Main populations, press inferences

New York Times population (n = 477)	% of inferences	*The Times* population (n = 276)	% of inferences
Unspecified members of the public/nation	43.2%	Unspecified members of the public/nation	51.4%
People from specific town/area	27.9%	Tory Party members/grassroots	9.8%
Consumers/shoppers	4.8%	People from specific town/area	6.5%
Investors	2.5%	Young people	5.4%
Young people	2.3%	Nurses and doctors	3.6%
Israeli public	1.9%	Pensioners, train passengers, business people, women, men (each)	1.8%

Not surprisingly, most inferences are made about the general public, or 'unspecified members of the public/nation'. This category refers to references that construct an 'imagined community' (Anderson, 1991) based on public opinion around a particular issue. For example, a story from *The Times* implies national unity around a concern for the health of key England football players. In it, the journalist suggests that 'the country will wince every time Michael Owen so much as breaks a fingernail between now and what should be the final match of the qualifying campaign' (*The Times*, 7th September 2001, sports section).

The second most frequent population is people from a specific town or area. This is a complicated category because the inferences about public opinion here work in at least two different ways. Sometimes they represent a community that is newsworthy in its own right – as when journalists sought out the opinion of New Yorkers in the wake of September 11th, and Afghani citizens after the fall of the Taliban. The prominence of this type of inference is consistent with Gans's (1980: 13–15) view that 'regular people' appear most frequently in the news when they are swept up in the tide of ongoing news events. Sometimes, however, an inference about the public opinion of people in a specific area is used as an indicator of broader public opinion trends. In the following story about the beleaguered state of the US economy, a CBS report on Michigan Avenue shoppers is used to illustrate a wider set of trends among American consumers:

> Along Michigan Avenue, the same jitters people are feeling about their security are now showing up in their spending at levels even people in the retail business find unnerving.
>
> *Mr Britt Beemer (America's Research Group)*: 'I've never seen a time when so many Americans have no interest at all in buying anything except going to the grocery store or going to their druggists to get their prescriptions.'
>
> (CBS News, 20th September 2001)

In this case, shoppers on Michigan Avenue in Chicago come to stand in for shoppers in the nation as a whole. While the individual Chicago consumers are not newsworthy in and of themselves, the story of American consumers neglecting their responsibilities was high on the news agenda after September 11th.[3] Indeed, our tables reveal that consumers and shoppers were the third most frequent population about whom inferences were made in the US and UK television samples, as well as in the *New York Times*.

By looking at the other main populations whose opinion is inferred, we can detect some interesting differences between the news agendas in the USA and the UK. The US television sample includes frequent inferences about the public opinion of Muslims and Arabs (4.5%) and air passengers (4.5%). This reflects the wealth of stories about the war in Afghanistan and the feelings of Muslims about it, as well as concerns about air safety in the wake of September 11th. The UK television sample reflects a different set of concerns: sports fans and parents, both important audiences, make up 5.7% and 4.7% of the inferences population, respectively.

In both the US and UK television samples, nurses and doctors make up 2.4% of the population whose opinion is inferred, reflecting a growing concern about their working conditions in both countries. By contrast, the *New York Times* includes a large number of inferences about the public opinion of investors (2.5%), informed by worries about the state of the economy. The Israeli public also makes an appearance in the top six of *New York Times* populations (1.9% of inferences), demonstrating that the Middle East remains central to the news agenda of US media in general, and the *New York Times* in particular (see Gamson, 1992; Christison, 2001). Both the *New York Times* and *The Times* contain a relatively high number of inferences to the public opinion of young people – 2.3% and 5.4%, respectively. This is probably because the newspaper sample is heavily weighted towards polling data, and young people are frequently polled separately. We speculate that the prevalence of such inferences may also be a product of growing concerns about young people's engagement with politics and society (see Buckingham, 2000).

However, Tables 6.7 and 6.8 do not even begin to describe the diversity of populations whose opinion is inferred. Inferences about the opinions of groups such as farmers, patients, teachers and drivers all contribute to constructing a complex image of the citizenry and its viewpoints. Even if public opinion is a 'visible fiction', often constructed in the interest of national unity, the variety of populations whose opinions are represented through inferences demonstrates the recognition that each issue, rather than affecting everyone equally, has particular stakeholders whose lives may be changed by decisions and events. For instance, in a CBS story on Bush's measure to introduce armed marshals on airplanes, the reporter suggested that 'that's what pilots want, guns in the cockpit' (26th September 2001). In this case, the opinion of pilots is integral to the news story, providing the appearance of balance and an assessment of policy proposals from those affected by it.[4]

Another story, this one from the *New York Times*, looks at reactions on the Greek island of Cephalonia to the book and film *Captain Corelli's Mandolin*. The book, set on the island, became a major Hollywood vehicle, featuring Nicholas Cage and Penelope Cruz. However, islanders are not impressed with the book, which in their opinion fails to represent historical events adequately:

> ... the latter-day leftists who are in the majority vehemently dispute its English author's unambiguous view of Greek partisans as thugs and Nazi collaborators.

> They are aghast at its sympathetic view of the prewar right-wing
> Greek dictator, Gen. Ioannis Metaxas, and outraged that there is no
> mention of the Greek Jews saved by the Communists.
>
> (*New York Times*, 21st August 2001, section E, page 1)

In support of such inferences about the public opinion of Cephalonians, this
story also contains a series of interviews with inhabitants of the island. It seeks
to redress what is often a fundamental problem in popular culture representations: that of the lack of a voice for those who are represented. Indeed, the film
version of *Captain Corelli's Mandolin* has been singled out for criticism by
media scholars, who argue that it represents a form of 'contemporary orientalism' (Tzanelli, 2003). The *New York Times* story reminds us that by including
overlooked perspectives and opinions, the media can serve as a progressive
social force, giving voice to social formations whose opinions matter, but
whose existence doesn't usually register on the radar of elite politics.

Inferences about public opinion are thus complicated creatures. On the
one hand, when they imply a unitary national public opinion, they are often
mobilised to tell a simplified story, and to prop up ideological and moral
arguments. On the other hand, they can work to give voice to stakeholders
who are necessary both for the balance of a story, and, more normatively, for
the adequate representation of the diversity of opinion. If the public sphere is a
site for individuals to discuss and settle matters of common concern, any discussion ought to endeavour to include the perspectives of all those affected by
a particular issue (Habermas, 1989: 27). Inferences about public opinion shed
light on the variety of perspectives and therefore contribute to what Rawls
(1997) has referred to as 'ideal role-taking': the ability to put yourself in other
people's shoes. However, as Habermas reminds us, merely imagining the viewpoints of others, as journalists do when they make inferences, is not enough;
what 'is needed is a "real" process of argumentation in which the individuals
concerned cooperate' (1989: 67). If we don't consult others, we will never
know what they really think. We can merely guess, but our guesses will be
informed by our own feelings, biases and preconceptions.

What are the inferences about?

Given that inferences about public opinion play such key roles in contextualising and interpreting news and views, it is interesting to see whether they
systematically appear in certain contexts, and equally, whether they are absent
from others. As Salwen (1995) has argued in the context of stories about disasters, citizens and their opinions are often taken seriously as news sources on
topics where they have a 'countervailing power' in relation to claims made by
official sources. For instance, in stories about natural disaster, the ' "power" of

individuals quoted in the news was that their pleas had to be considered in the political context of disaster' (Salwen, 1995: 836). Some of Salwen's observations are played out in our sample, as demonstrated in Tables 6.9 and 6.10.

What is notable about the distribution of inferences and unspecified inferences is that the dominant topics are somewhat different from those characterising our overall sample, discussed in Chapter 3. There is certainly considerable overlap – for both inferences and the sample overall, topics such as September 11th, Afghanistan, terrorism and crime play key roles. However, the specified and unspecified inferences are frequently about politics and government, and about the economy, business and employment. Where does this imbalance stem from? One explanation is that stories about politics and the economy have a reputation among journalists for being uninteresting to their audiences (see Haahr and Holm, 2003, ch. 3). They may be seen as distant and irrelevant to their daily lives, whereas audiences are assumed to be interested primarily in local issues that affect them directly. By including inferences about public opinion in a story about politics or the economy, the impact of

Table 6.9   Main topics of inferences about public opinion[a]

	US TV (n = 1,232)	UK TV (n = 674)	*New York Times* (n = 477)	*The Times* (n = 276)
Politics and government	2.2%	4.7%	35.0%	34.0%
Economy/business/ employment	5.9%	4.9%	7.3%	7.6%
September 11th/scares and fears[b]	32.0%	9.0%	5.9%	4.4%
Afghanistan[c]	15.1%	9.4%	3.6%	8.0%
Terrorism and terrorists[d]	13.7%	5.1%	3.5%	1.8%
Public services[e]	3.4%	17.1%	4.4%	11.6
Crime	0.9%	5.5%	3.6%	4.3%
Europe	0.1%	3.7%	4.2%	5.4%
Sport/entertainment	1.8%	9.2%	2.6%	3.6%
Consumption/shopping	7.0%	6.4%	7.8%	1.8%

a. This table includes all subjects that made up more than 1% of the vox pop sample for either US or UK in TV or newspapers. Subjects included in the category of 'other', which are too small to feature in the table, include attitudes towards the USA, the conflict in Kashmir, festivals, fishing, charities and past wars.

b. This category includes references to the mood after September 11th, anthrax, national security and air travel safety.

c. Includes references to the US attack on Afghanistan, the future of Afghanistan, the Taliban and the humanitarian situation in the country.

d. Includes references to terrorism, terrorists and more specific references to Osama bin Laden.

e. Includes stories on health services, education, railways, social security and pensions/retirement.

Table 6.10   Main topics of unspecified inferences

	US TV (n = 276)	UK TV (n = 206)	New York Times (n = 148)	The Times (n = 96)
Politics and government	6.5%	8.2%	35.8%	26.0%
Economy/business/ employment	5.4%	2.9%	8.1%	13.6%
September 11th/scares and fears[a]	22.0%	2.5%	5.5%	1.0%
Afghanistan[b]	10.5%	7.3%	3.4%	0.0%
Terrorism and terrorists[c]	13.8%	3.9%	0.7%	1.0%
Public services[d]	4.0%	17.5%	2.8%	5.2%
Crime	1.8%	8.7%	1.4%	3.1%
Sport/entertainment	2.8%	9.8%	11.5%	27.1%
Environment	0.0%	1.5%	5.4%	1.0%
Natural disasters or accidents	1.8%	5.3%	0.0%	0.0%

a. Includes references to the mood after September 11th, anthrax, national security and air travel safety.
b. Includes references to the US attack on Afghanistan, the future of Afghanistan, the Taliban and the humanitarian situation in the country.
c. Includes references to terrorism, terrorists and more specific references to Osama bin Laden.
d. Includes stories on health services, education, railways and pensions/retirement.

events on regular people's lives can be dramatically illustrated, and the story can therefore be made relevant to a wider audience. For example, in an ITV story on Gordon Brown's pre-Budget statement, the correspondent inferred that 'pensioners in Cardiff were unimpressed' with the pension allocations described in the statement (ITV News, 27 November 2001).

While we have no systematic evidence comparing the types of stories on which public opinion was referenced to those on which it was not, we can piece together a couple of observations about contexts in which public opinion was seen as essential to the news story. As we will discuss in more detail in Chapter 7 (on September 11th), in the US sample, public opinion was widely present in stories about September 11th and its aftermath, while in Britain many stories reporting on the success and failure of public services drew on public opinion references of all types. On the other hand, an examination of television news transcripts[5] indicates that public opinion is usually absent from particular types of stories. These include political 'insider' stories, such as ones about changes in Tony Blair's Cabinet, the candidacy for the position of First Minister of the Scottish Parliament, and controversies around then British Transport Minister Stephen Byers. They also include stories about ongoing criminal cases, such as murder cases, burglaries, rapes, cases of doctors struck off the register for misconduct, as well as stories about military exercises and movements. These are stories that unfold in a realm outside the influence of public opinion. Having said that, the overrepresentation of inferences – the easiest, briefest form of reference to public opinion – in stories about politics and the economy might indicate that the views of citizens are increasingly considered integral to the news agenda as a whole.

Conclusion

If mass communication is a system of representation through which citizen-ship is expressed (see Dahlgren, 1995; Calabrese, 2001: 151), inferences about public opinion – whether they refer to a specific population or an unspecified group – play a central role in contextualising such expressions. This chapter has examined the role of inferences in news stories, and sought to understand the nature of the claims they make about public opinion.

Our data show that inferences are by far the most common type of refer-ence to public opinion – the two types discussed in this chapter make up the majority of references in our sample. At the same time, they are also the most off-hand way of referring to the citizenry. They require no systematic evidence or support, and sometimes have more bearing on the beliefs of journalists than on the views of the public (see King and Schudson, 1995; Sumpter, 2000). Inferences are usually made by journalists, and work to easily characterise – and therefore unify – what is in reality a messy and diverse body of public opinion. They appear to allow citizen deliberation to construct the news agenda, but do not actually involve any citizens. While expert viewpoints on public opinion are constructed as factual and legitimate, politicians' state-ments are viewed with suspicion and faced with criticism.

Inferences rarely appear as the sole mention of public opinion in a story. They are usually followed by other types of references – usually vox pop interviews, or, in rarer cases, images of demonstrations or evidence from pub-lic opinion polls. Indeed, unspecified inferences often simply play the role of introducing the presence of countervailing viewpoints, providing balance to the story. For this reason, the categories discussed in this chapter cannot be viewed in isolation, but should be seen as part of a larger trend towards more faithfully representing public opinion.

Indeed, the chapter has also shown that while inferences about public opinion can be sweeping and refer to an imagined national public, journalists are often careful to specify the population whose opinion is inferred – whether it be young people, air passengers or farmers – and endeavour to reflect the diversity of public opinion. Similarly, inferences about more specific groups within the nation often serve to highlight how these groups are affected by events, illustrating the significance of what can otherwise be dull and inaccessible stories. Although inferences usually do little to capture any real evidence of public opinion, they arguably infuse our news media with the sense that citizens matter to the political process.

Notes

1.   These figures are total figures, combining the US and UK samples, and also based on the aggregate of figures for 'Politician at home' and 'Politician in other country'.
2.   This variable was only coded for the inferences about public opinion – by their very nature, unspecified inferences do not refer to a particular population.
3.   For a more detailed discussion of this point, see Chapter 7.
4.   Note, however, that a later ITV story (31st October 2001) provided evidence of European pilots' resistance to armed air marshals – apparently, then, the public opinion of pilots inferred by the CBS reporter does not reflect the views of pilots around the world.
5.   For the UK television sample, we kept a running log of all stories on each programme. This log was compared with our record of stories containing references to public opinion. In the case of ITV News, this was done for the whole sample period, while for the BBC sample, this was only done for the period 11th January 2001–11th February 2001.

7 Public opinion in crisis
September 11th and its aftermath

If it is the role of the news media to show their audiences how to be active citizens, then the aftermath of September 11th, maybe more than ever, was a time to rise to the challenge. While emotions ran high, the USA and its allies embarked on a global war on terror. Citizens' participation in the debate over how to respond to a terrorist attack would have been crucial to the democratic process of decision making. In this chapter we explore the extent to which, at a time of crisis, US and British news media reminded citizens that while nations mourned, political actions were to be debated. For our discussion we look primarily at the representation of public opinion on the following subjects: terrorism, the mood after September 11th, anthrax and the military attacks on Afghanistan. The social, political and military aftermath of September 11th was *the* story at the time. It is likely that the data of our total sample period have been influenced by the dominance of this single issue. Yet it is because news reporting in the immediate aftermath of September 11th is not representative of normal patterns of news reporting that our data allow us to explore how news media represent public opinion during a 'national crisis'. Observers of US media have already highlighted some patterns of reporting that have emerged: a sidelining of voices critical of government policy, as well as a negative portrayal of Muslim citizens, has been identified (Schurr, 2001; McChesney, 2002). Our analysis taps into this debate: we pick up on concerns raised in previous chapters and explore the extent to which citizens were represented as active participants of the public sphere. Further, we ask whether news reporting offered a range of political viewpoints and an international debate. Our findings suggest that at a time of crisis, news media do not necessarily break with patterns they follow at 'normal' times. Yet, while keeping up established practices, they also cast citizens in ways that at other times are less pronounced. We explore these more unusual practices: we discuss how an emphasis on citizens' emotional reactions created the image of a citizenry incapable of setting the political agenda, and how shopping appeared as the only available form of active citizenship.

Our data suggest that news media certainly gave the public a platform to express their views, about the experience of September 11th, as well as about the war on terror. Both US and British news frequently referred to public opinion on the mood after September 11th, terrorism, anthrax and the military attacks on Afghanistan. In our television sample these topics are among the six most frequently occurring subjects of public opinion references. In our newspaper sample these subjects do not appear as frequently as in television news, yet nevertheless rank among the nineteen most frequently appearing subjects of public opinion.[1] Yet while both US and British news frequently referred to public opinion, they did not create the image of a citizenry seeking to set the political agenda on these issues.

On the subjects of terrorism and military attacks on Afghanistan, we compared the following four broad levels of citizenship engagement, introduced in Chapter 3:

1. Citizens making proposals (in the form of an appeal to government/ corporate world/fellow citizens).
2. Citizens responding to politicians.
3. Citizens commenting on issue/event/group without making proposals for action.
4. Citizens speaking about personal experiences or as consumers.

Representations of citizens who make clear proposals create the sense that they actively participate in the public sphere: they are aware of social and political issues, formulate an opinion and propose a course of action. We have defined such representations as the most active level of citizenship. It is here that we can see citizens making suggestions about what should be done in the world, either by governments, the corporate world, or fellow citizens. It is through such references, like the following examples, that news media create the image of a public that actively seeks to set the political agenda, instead of being acted upon by political elites:

> Afghan people 'are asking for more and more international troops'.
> (BBC, 31st January 2002)

> *Unidentified woman*: 'I mean, Americans should be more politicised. They should know – know more about what's going on in other regions.'
> (NBC News, 22nd October 2001)

However, in both US and British television news such references were rare.[2] More frequent were examples of citizens responding to politicians and parties:

Mr Rove told Republican candidates at the weekend that 'we can go to the country on this issue of the war on terrorism' because voters trusted Republicans to do a better job 'protecting America'.

(*The Times*, 21st January 2002)

In these references we do not get to see members of the public proposing a course of action. Nevertheless, we see them formulating an opinion about political issues. They thus are part of the public sphere. On British television news this is the nature of citizen expression that appears most frequently. This could suggest that at least on British television news there was an attempt to represent citizens as members of the public sphere. However, even though these references suggest that citizens have an opinion on politics, they do not imply that they actively seek to shape the course of political action. It is only through references that show citizens making clear proposals, that news media create the sense of a (by our definition) truly deliberative participation in the public sphere. Yet, in both US and British television samples, these most active forms of citizen engagement were the least frequently appearing category. This suggests that overall neither British nor US television showed citizens as actively engaged. Instead, they represented them as following a political process, which is not set by them. This image of citizens as passive members of the public sphere is sharpened by the high percentage of references that show citizens commenting on social issues or events:[3]

A group of New York firefighters and policemen showed up in Kabul today to deliver a shipment of aid to an orphanage in the capital. And here they are in the first person.

Unidentified man: 'This is full circle. We just left ground zero, in New York, and travel for two days to come to ground zero here in Afghanistan. We're very proud to be here. Right now I'm looking at a lot of children without fathers back in New York. Their – their fathers' lives were snuffed away from them. So it's no different here than anywhere else. Maybe these kids don't have any parents. And we want to put a smile on their face, especially during Christmas time. Why not? That's what it's all about.'

(ABC News, 21st December 2001)

These frequently appearing forms of citizens' participation in the public sphere represent a civic community whose members are aware of social issues. However, they do not further the impression that this community actively seeks to shape the political agenda. Citizens are shown as non-deliberative members of the public sphere. Thus it can be argued that public debate on subjects related to September 11th were depoliticised, in both US and British news.[4] Citizens had little opportunity to set the agenda of debate.

These findings correspond with the pattern of reporting we discussed in previous chapters: news media mainly represent the image of a passive public, whose main form of participation in the public sphere is, at best, following the agenda set by political leaders.

The representation of public opinion on subjects related to September 11th highlights another general practice of news reporting: the sidelining of liberal and left-wing opinions. As we argue in Chapter 3, US and British news media reinforce the image of a generally conservative public. The diverse range of opinions held by the public at large is not represented. This general imbalance in the representation of citizens' political views shows in news coverage of the war on terror and the military attacks on Afghanistan. On the subject of terrorism, for example, over 90% of references to public opinion in television news cannot be classified in ideological terms. The political voices we do get to see are predominantly right-wing (thirty-two references, compared to one count of left-wing opinions). Consequently an image of a generally traditional and conservative public emerges. Thus, not only does the public appear little engaged in active political debate, but they also appear supportive of a conservative agenda. As the conservative US administration took the lead in international politics, both US and British news media fell in line by shutting out alternative ideological positions.

Another general, 'everyday' practice of news reporting that shows in the reporting of issues relating to September 11th, is the extent to which news media gave room to citizens' opinions from all over the world. The consequences of the 'global war on terror' (Coalition Information Centers, 2001) were felt not just by Britain and the USA, but by an international coalition and the countries it targeted. The representation of public opinion at home *and* abroad would have contributed to the sense that here was an international public debate on an issue of international concern. Yet after September 11th, news media did not break with established patterns of reporting. As we argue in Chapter 2, British news overall carries more references to public opinion abroad than US news. This practice also shows in the representation of public opinion on September 11th-related issues. In British news, the sense of an international public debate could emerge. In contrast, US news did not present these issues as matters where public opinion outside the USA was of much significance. In particular on the subject of terrorism, US television news, for instance, focused primarily on public opinion at home. Over 90% of references to citizens' opinions on the subject of terrorism were opinions held by people in the USA. This emphasis on public opinion at home partly reflects the extent to which the war on terror is a US-led story. Yet at the same time it also reflects the general practice of US news to emphasise the national angle of news stories. In Chapter 2 we highlighted how, as a consequence, US news in general tends to represent

Table 7.1 The proportion of different levels of citizen engagement on the subject of military attacks on Afghanistan on television and in the press

	US TV (n = 238)	UK TV (n = 87)	TV total (n = 325)	New York Times (n = 55)	The Times (n = 63)	Total (n = 118)
Appeals to government/corporate world/fellow citizens	10.5%	2.3%	8.3%	58.2%	47.6%	52.5%
Response to politicians	36.6%	65.5%	44.3%	16.4%	33.3%	25.4%
Discussing social issue/event	47.5%	29.9%	42.8%	23.6%	17.5%	20.3%
Private individual speaks from own experience, or as consumer	5.5%	2.3%	4.6%	1.8%	1.6%	1.7%

Table 7.2 The proportion of different levels of citizen engagement on the subject of terrorism/treatment of terrorists on television[a] and in the press[b]

	US TV (n = 297)	UK TV (n = 51)	TV total (n = 348)	New York Times (n = 27)	The Times (n = 10)	Total (n = 37)
Appeals to government/corporate world/ fellow citizens	3.7%	2.0%	3.4%	22.2%	0.0%	16.2%
Response to politics and parties	7.4%	9.8%	7.8%	22.2%	10.0%	18.9%
Discussing social issue/event	63.6%	74.5%	65.2%	55.6%	90.0%	64.9%
Private individual speaks from own experience, or as consumer	25.3%	13.7%	23.6%			

a. Chi-square tests suggested that US/UK differences for cases where these could be tested (expected cell count at least 5) were not statistically significant (p = 0.071). Differences within the US sample were statistically significant (p < 0.05). Differences within the UK sample, for cases were these could be tested (expected cell count at least 5), were statistically significant (p = 0.022).
b. Chi-square tests suggested that US/UK differences, for cases were these could be tested (expected cell count at least 5) were not statistically significant (p = 051). Differences within the US sample for cases where these could be tested (expected cell count at least 5) were statistically significant (p < 0.05). Differences within the UK sample could not be tested.

an inward-looking public debate. Our data on the war on terrorism suggest that, at a time when US policy had profound effects on other countries, US news media sustained their general practice of shutting out international opinion.

The representation of public opinion on subjects related to September 11th thus shows the same general patterns of news reporting we explore in other chapters: we rarely get to see citizens who are actively trying to set the agenda of political debate. We get to see the image of a conservative public, and in the case of US news, an inward-looking debate.

Yet as we suggested earlier, news coverage at a time of crisis produced more than the usual patterns of reporting. One of these 'peculiarities' of news coverage in the aftermath of September 11th is the frequent representation of citizens who talk about their feelings in relation to the events of September 11th, anthrax, terrorism and military attacks on Afghanistan. For most of our analysis of different forms of citizen engagement we have folded references to citizens' emotional reactions into a broader category of references, which accounts for all cases where we see citizens discussing social events or issues, without making a proposal about a course of action. References in this category, such as the example of New York fire fighters quoted above, show citizens as passive members of the public sphere: even though they discuss social events or issues, they do not make a proposal about a course of action. There are subtle differences between the ways we see citizens discussing a social issue. For our analysis of subjects relating to September 11th, it is worth unpacking them. The following examples illustrate the difference between an emotional reaction and a non-emotional response to the same issue, the war in Afghanistan. In the first example, we see a veteran commenting on the US army and its performance. In the second, we see how a Pakistani civilian's emotional reaction led him to commit himself to retaliation.

> At 80 years old, he has – he has a lot of wisdom, a lot to offer. The wisdom that America can prevail, now needed more than ever, as his country fights a different kind of war in Afghanistan.
>
> *Mr Whetstine*: 'There's no other country's got a fighting force like us. We're gonna win.'
>
> (NBC News, 12th December 2001)

> Twenty-year-old Mohammed Ishaq plans to go to Afghanistan to fight US troops.
>
> *Mr Ishaq*: 'I'm – I'm ready to give my life.'
>
> He and his friends listen to the BBC every night and what they hear has driven them to militancy.

Table 7.3 The proportion of references to public opinion at home versus references to public opinion abroad on television and in the press

	US TV (n = 2,880)	UK TV (n = 1,518)	TV total (n = 4,398)	New York Times (n = 1,679)	The Times (n = 1,023)	Press total (n = 2,720)
Military attacks on Afghanistan	USA	UK	Total	New York Times	The Times	Press total
Home	41.6%	27.6%	37.8%	90.9%	54.0%	71.2%
Abroad	58.4%	72.4%	62.2%	9.1%	46.0%	28.8%
Mood after September 11th	USA	UK	Total	New York Times	The Times	Total
Home	92.2%	3.4%	86.9%	92.0%	18.2%	78.7%
Abroad	7.8%	96.6%	13.1%	8.0%	81.8%	21.3%
Terrorism/treatment of terrorists	USA	UK	Total	New York Times	The Times	Total
Home	91.9%	45.1%	85.1%	77.8%	40.0%	67.6%
Abroad	8.1%	54.9%	14.9%	22.2%	60.0%	32.4%
Anthrax	USA	UK	Total	New York Times	The Times	Total
Home	100.0%	14.3%	96.5%	–	–	–
Abroad	0.0%	85.7%	3.5%	–	–	–
Other	USA	UK	Total	New York Times	The Times	Total
Home	78.3%	79.7%	78.9%	74.2%	75.3%	74.6%
Abroad	21.7%	20.3%	21.1%	25.8%	24.7%	25.4%

Mr Ishaq: 'They are very angry because – with America and British. They're really angry.'

(CBS News, 6th November 2001)

Mohammed Ishaq's statement, while a form of participation in the public sphere, appears to be based less on reason and an informed knowledge of social and political issues. He also seems less capable of forming an objective opinion than the veteran, who at least speaks about the military from the perspective of an insider. While we, as the audience, might suspect the veteran of having a nostalgic view of the US army, his quote and the reporter's voice-over do not push this interpretation. He seems more rational than the man in Pakistan. Similarly, the following statement by a British civilian does not work as an example of citizens' balanced and considerate engagement with the issue in question:

All across Europe, from Paris to Brussels, Lockerbie to Lisbon, the events of one single day produced a single reaction: to turn tears into resolve.

Prime Minister Tony Blair (Great Britain): 'We, therefore, here in Britain, stand shoulder to shoulder with our American friends in this hour of tragedy.'

And they stood on the streets, too.

Unidentified man: 'One's initial reaction is to just go and nail the bastards.'

(CBS News, 31st December 2001)

Even though his statement is loosely connected to the possibility of military retaliation, he does not make a clear proposal about what should be done. He speaks about his 'initial reaction', and does not make a clear statement about who should attack whom, and possibly how. His reaction is purely emotional. Had he made a clear proposal about what should be done, this would have been an example of a citizen deliberatively participating in the public sphere. By distinguishing emotional reactions from all other forms of citizen engagement, we can determine the extent to which news media created the image of a public whose deliberative participation in the public sphere is stifled by emotions. In making the distinction between emotional reactions and other forms of citizen engagement, we do not wish to argue that proposals about political (or military) action cannot be influenced by, or caused by, an emotional reaction. Similarly, comments on social issues can be driven by emotions. Yet we do suggest that an emphasis on emotions diminishes the sense that citizens' participation in the public sphere is informed by a balanced and rational awareness of political and social issues.

Our data on emotional reactions are particularly interesting in relation to the subjects of terrorism and the military attacks on Afghanistan. These are issues that can be expected to trigger emotional responses. Yet at the same time, they are clearly tied to political debate, such as the decision over whether to opt for military or diplomatic action after September 11th. We coded personal expressions of fear, as well as comments on governments' decisions on the war on terror, as opinions on the subjects of terrorism. Similarly, expressions of feelings, as well as comments on political decisions relating to this specific aspect of US foreign policy, would fall under the subject category of military attacks on Afghanistan. On both of these potentially political subjects, there is a high frequency of references to citizens reacting emotionally (on the subject of terrorism over 30% of references, for example).

The strong emphasis on emotions in both US and British news, at the expense of references to rational public debate, created the sense of a civic community that was not ready, or in any state, to take the pressure of national crisis and make rational proposals about what should be done. As we discuss earlier in this and other chapters, our data suggest that US and British news only rarely show citizens deliberatively participating in the public sphere. The emphasis on citizens' emotions on subjects relating to September 11th gives this image of a passive public a seemingly natural explanation. This image of an almost irrational and headless public was particularly pronounced in US news media, and especially in the representation of citizens at home, in the USA. British news media were more likely to refer to citizens abroad as emotional, rather than citizens at home. The image of an emotion-laden debate abroad thus contrasts with the image of a more cool-headed public at home. US news, in contrast, stressed the emotional struggles of citizens at home. As we argued earlier in this chapter, at the same time they sustained the image of a generally conservative public. Thus, the emphasis

Table 7.4 The proportion of emotional responses (compared with all other levels of citizen engagement) on television and in the press

	US TV (n = 2,880)	UK TV (n = 1,518)	New York Times (n = 1,679)	The Times (n = 1,023)
Military attacks on Afghanistan	17.6%	16.1%	14.5%	11.1%
Mood after September 11th	37.7%	41.4%	28.0%	54.5%
Terrorism/treatment of terrorists	33.0%	33.3%	25.9%	20.0%
Anthrax	38.6%	71.4%	0.0%	0.0%
Other	11.9%	9.8%	4.7%	1.7%

on citizens' emotions and their supposedly conservative values creates the sense that the decisions of a conservative government seem naturally uncontested.

Moreover, even when citizens were represented as being aware of policies and debates, their participation in the public sphere sometimes was presented as motivated by emotions. Again the sense of rationality behind citizens' engagement in the political debate is diminished. A look at references to citizens' responses to political leaders and their actions in US news suggests that even some of these comments on politics were emotionally driven:

> But most Americans said they were favorably impressed, at times even emotionally moved, by Mr. Bush. In Longmont, Colo., a dozen customers at Riley's restaurant listened intently to the speech, applauding occasionally amid a small forest of American flags stuck in empty beer pitchers. 'Bush is like his dad, he has a big heart,' said Cyndi Morris, a painter and artist. 'I believe God has sent us an ark in Bush. We're all going to get through this together, side by side. I feel a lot better after hearing him. I think he knows how to pull us together.'
>
> (*New York Times*, 21st September 2001)

> Merle Gross, 59, a manufacturer of women's clothing, said in Chicago that she agreed with much of what Mr. Bush said but called him a 'flawed communicator' who had missed a crucial opportunity. 'He just doesn't have the passion,' she said. 'He's just not convincing. I couldn't buy a car from him. The default expression on his face is such an unfortunate one. I hope that I'm not a typical American in my response.'
>
> (*New York Times*, 21st September 2001)

Apart from an emphasis on emotions, particularly US news coverage shows another peculiarity in the reporting on issues relating to September 11th. Qualitative analysis of news reporting suggests that consumerism became defined as a form of active citizenship. In our definition of different forms of citizen engagement we did not consider consumerism as a participation in the public sphere. References that show citizens speaking as consumers have been coded as expressions of personal experience. Yet a qualitative analysis of references to citizens who speak as consumers shows that news media defined shopping as a way in which citizens could make an active contribution to the well-being of their national community. Consumerism became defined as an active form of citizen engagement.

The idea that citizenship can be expressed in civic activism has a long tradition in the United States (Kalberg, 1993: 98–100). A broad view of

Table 7.5 The proportion of emotional responses by citizens at home versus emotional responses of citizens abroad on television and in the press

	US TV (n = 582)	UK TV (n = 180)	TV Total (n = 762)	New York Times (n = 102)	The Times (n = 31)	Press total (n = 133)
Military attacks on Afghanistan	US TV	UK TV	TV total	New York Times	The Times	Press total
Home	33.3%	14.3%	28.6%	75.0%	14.3%	46.7%
Abroad	66.7%	85.7%	71.4%	25.0%	85.7%	53.3%
Mood after September 11th	US TV	UK TV	TV total	New York Times	The Times	Press total
Home	90.8%	8.3%	85.4%	92.9%	16.7%	70.0%
Abroad	9.2%	91.7%	14.6%	7.1%	83.3%	30.0%
Terrorism/treatment of terrorists	US TV	UK TV	TV total	New York Times	The Times	Press total
Home	93.9%	23.5%	83.5%	71.4%	0.0%	55.6%
Abroad	6.1%	76.5%	16.5%	28.6%	100%	44.4%
Anthrax	US TV	UK TV	TV total	New York Times	The Times	Press total
Home	100%	0.0%	92.8%	0.0%	0.0%	0.0%
Abroad	0.0%	100%	7.2%	0.0%	0.0%	0.0%
Other	USA	UK	Total	New York Times	The Times	Total
Home	77.6%	69.7%	74.5%	42.5%	43.8%	42.7%
Abroad	22.4%	30.3%	25.5%	57.5%	56.3%	57.3%

citizenship as involving more than political and civil rights emerged in the early United States. Citizenship 'became understood as implying an entire spectrum of activities beyond the casting of votes', such as writing letters to Congresspersons and participation in political parties and campaigns (Kalberg, 1993: 100). Such participation in community life has a purpose beyond individual self-interest. The individual contributes to the greater good of all. With the emergence of consumerism and the advertising industry, the ethos of self-denial was supplanted by an ethos of personal fulfilment. The promise of mass consumption became central to the idea of freedom and an entitlement to citizenship in the USA (Foner, 1998: 147–8). Access to consumer goods came close to being considered a civic right. Not to have access to mass consumption, to be excluded from this promise of a consumerist America, was considered almost as serious a social issue as the exclusion from the right to vote had previously been (*ibid.*). Consumers became an important social voice. Consumerism sparked not just political activism, but also a sense of belonging. Access to the world of consumer goods that signal prosperity and social achievement became central to the concept of US national identity. Cold War rhetoric exploited this idea, putting the freedom of free enterprise and a high standard of living at the heart of what it means to enjoy 'American values' and the 'American way of life' (Foner, 1998: 270–2). Consumption is turned into the goal of the nation-state and the fulfilment of the democratic aspirations of its people. Thus consumerism today is central to the idea of what it means to be American. Yet while consumerism bears the potential for collective social action and comes close to being considered a civic right, it is not a civic duty. This was to change with the events of September 11th, when 'good' civic participation became aligned with consumerism. The equation of active citizenship with consumerism was part of government rhetoric. George W. Bush called upon citizens to keep the economy going:

> We must be steadfast. We must be resolved. We must not let the terrorists cause our nation to stop traveling, to stop buying, to stop living ordinary lives.
>
> (remarks by the President to Military Personnel Travis
> Air Force Base, California, www.whitehouse.gov/news/
> releases/2001/10/20011017-20.html)

Capitalist enterprise was put at the heart of US identity. Resistance against critics of this system and its 'way of life' was best expressed by sustaining consumerism. Government rhetoric defined shopping as an act that would express US national identity. In this equation, defiance of consumerism becomes a way of excluding oneself from the national community. Actively resisting the message of consumerism meant being placed in the same category as 'them', the terrorists who attacked 'a symbol of American prosperity':

> I ask your continued participation and confidence in the American economy. Terrorists attacked a symbol of American prosperity. They did not touch its source. America is successful because of the hard work, and creativity, and enterprise of our people. These were the true strengths of our economy before September 11th, and they are our strengths today.
>
> (address to a Joint Session of Congress and the American People, United States Capitol, Washington, DC, www.whitehouse. gov/news/releases/2001/09/20010920-8.html)

In order to create the link between shopping and patriotism, government rhetoric did not need to construct an entirely new idea. As argued above, Cold War rhetoric made consumerism central to US identity. Today US business seeks to cash in on patriotically motivated consumption. Products that feed the everyday imagining of the nation through 'banal nationalism' (Billig, 1995) have already been widely available prior to the terrorist attacks. What many of these products have in common is a use of the US flag, which is turned into an everyday accessory of national identity (Marvin and Ingle, 1999: 29). Online shops, such as the 'America Store' of Larose.com (www.larose.com/America/) offer a wealth of products with which to 'flag the homeland daily' (Billig, 1995) and to signal national belonging in our everyday lives. After September 11th the range of products was widened and included products that tied symbols of the nation (the US flag and eagle in particular) to the Twin Towers and the terrorist attacks. The fashion company DKNY, for example, advertised its flag-adorned clothing together with the image of a crying model. Tear and flag combine to create a symbol of patriotism, which centres on the memory of national tragedy.

Through the act of consumption, the memory can be displayed on consumers' bodies. Thus after September 11th, business and government discourse aligned consumerism with US identity, and shopping became a patriotic duty. Our data suggest that news media sustained this discourse by presenting consumerism as a patriotic act. As we have argued in previous chapters, our data suggest that US news media in general emphasised citizens' consumer identities: 5.9% of all coded references in our US television sample, and 3.8% in our US newspaper sample, cast citizens in the role of consumers. A qualitative analysis of these references shows that they are part of a discourse that defined shopping as patriotic act. Consumerism became defined as a desirable, active contribution to one's national community. This is not to suggest that prior to September 11th news media presented consumer attitudes as having no effect on the country. Before September 11th, American consumers were represented as the key to a successful economy:

> Mitch Stapley, a money manager in Grand Rapids, Mich., said, 'The consumer is the last finger hanging on the edge of the cliff, and if we lose him,' he said, the economy could slip into recession.
>
> (*New York Times*, 8th August 2001)

Moreover, anxious consumers sometimes appeared as a threat to those in power. Dissatisfied consumers appeared in the role of voters who exercise their citizenship rights:

> There is no telling at this point exactly how the tax cut will affect Mr. Bush politically. That will more likely be determined by the performance of the economy than by any voter feelings about the tax cut per se. Mr. Reagan's approval ratings sank after he signed his tax cut because of the recession that followed.
>
> (*New York Times*, 8th June 2001)

Criticism of government economic policy is a clear indicator of political participation, even though it stops short of suggesting a course of political action. Consumption, however, is not. It appears as individualistic action that, by default, affects the rest of the national community. Moreover, it is represented neither as an action motivated by affection towards one's nation-state, nor as a moral obligation one has to perform for 'good citizen credentials'. Prior to September 11th what figured prominently was the assumption that the government should decide on a course of action and implement it accordingly. In short, the government was positioned as provider for the nations' citizens. If it failed to fulfil this role, citizens had the power and the right to make their disapproval known. Citizens appeared as a community of people with rights, more so than a community of people with common duties. They react to political and economic events.

September 11th represents a turning point in the way consumers were represented: consumer confidence and shopping were still presented as being vital to the success of the economy. Yet, incorporated into the discourse on the economy and recession was now the notion of patriotically motivated consumption. In vox pops American audiences got to see consumers motivated by a feeling of responsibility for the wider community:

> Even after a rough September, the auto industry is expecting its third best year ever. Atlanta dealer Eddie Bostwick says zero percent financing had customers back in force this past weekend.

> *Mr Eddie Bostwick*: 'The customers are – are feeling good about it. They
> know it's a good deal.'

It certainly made a buyer out of Verlin Sweat.

> *Mr Verlin Sweat*: 'I can buy a new vehicle and serve my purpose, as well
> as maybe help the economy a little bit.'
>
> > (ABC News, 2 October 2001)

After September 11th, shopping as participatory citizenship appeared as a
theme in articles and news bulletins on the state of the economy. It was also
embedded into stories on Americans' solidarity and charitable feelings after
the terrorist attacks. Consumption became incorporated into a narrative that
equated citizen identity with an awareness of community needs. One's 'good
citizen' credentials could be expressed by buying any symbol of American
cultural tradition. The 'hot items' of the year included 'anything that looks like
or tastes like America' (ABC World News Tonight, 18th September 2001). For
community-minded consumers who have more money at their disposal, the
range of products available also included shares in the stock market.

> Patriotism some thought dormant has been sprouting up all over in
> interesting ways . . . ballplayers in Chicago and some stock brokers
> who got new clients.
>
> *Unidentified man*: 'Who actually called me and felt it was their patri-
> otic duty to go out and buy American securities.'
> *Unidentified man*: 'A lot of people are donating to Red Cross. I'm going
> to try to help the economy a little bit by buying the stock.'
>
> > (ABC News, 18th September 2001)

Another product available to display one's solidarity with the national
community is the flag.

> Then, on the way home, I noticed that nearly every house I passed
> had hoisted an American flag to replace the usual Halloween goblins.
> The collective impulse made me feel less alone. But when I stopped in
> at the local hardware store to ask about flags, the owner said he had
> sold out that morning . . . All I knew was that the air smelled like fire
> and I wanted a big flag.
>
> > (*New York Times*, 20th September 2001)

Thus citizens were called into the shopping malls. Yet not every citizen seemed
to follow the call to spend. News media also represented these cautious consumers. As prior to September 11th, US news again constructed a link between
cautious consumer behaviour and recession:

Even before the terrorist attacks on the World Trade Center and the Pentagon, consumer confidence was down and merchants were preparing for the toughest holiday season in a decade. The assaults have thrown new questions into the planning and created an atmosphere in which what to sell and how to sell it have become highly charged issues.

(New York Times, 27th September 2001)

Yet these references to cautious consumers need to be placed in the context of news reporting that at the same time worked against consumers' worries by positioning them in the role of patriots. Spending money is represented as desirable social behaviour. Hurting financially means giving to the nation and performing one's civic role.

The elevation of shopping to a civic duty is particularly striking considering how the citizens' role was otherwise reduced to passive followers of politics. US and British news media created the image of a public that follows a political agenda set by those in government power. Despite mass demonstrations against US and British policy taking place all over the world, news media sidelined left-wing and liberal voices. In the USA, news media limited the balance of reporting even further, by focusing on public opinion at home. There was little space and airtime for the views of citizens in other countries, some of which would have to support or bear the brunt of the US-led military campaign. The paucity of examples that represent citizens ideologically opposing the conservative agenda is exacerbated by the scarcity of examples that show citizens making clear proposals about a course of action. Citizens mainly appear in the role of passive followers, who are acted upon. The positioning of citizens in this role is not exclusive to subjects relating to September 11th. What is different from references to public opinion on other subjects is the emphasis on citizens' emotions. Not only do citizens appear as followers of the political agenda, but they also appear as barely capable of doing anything else. Their reactions to policies and events appear driven by feelings, rather than rational thinking. What emerges is the impression of citizens being nearly incapable of taking the pressures of a national crisis and leadership. Instead of setting the political agenda, we see them pinning their hopes on strong leaders. By creating this image of a civic community paralysed by emotions, news media give a seemingly 'natural' explanation, and justification, for the representation of citizens as mere followers of the political process. It is only in the role of consumers that citizens appear as taking charge and actively participating in public life. Yet, while spending money was represented as an active form of citizenship, this performance of good citizenship was only active in the sense that it constituted an active compliance with the needs of a capitalist system. Even though they were shown expressing the wish to participate in public life, citizens were not represented as actively setting the agenda of political debate. After September 11th, news media placed the 'duty' to express patriotism through consumption before the need to participate actively and critically in the political process.

Notes

1. The sample period for our analysis of newspapers differs from the sample of television news in that it includes news published prior to 12th September. Further, only a small selection of keywords was used to identify relevant articles for our analysis ('poll'/'polls' and 'people think'). A comparison between our television and newspaper sample is difficult to make, yet it seems likely that the differences between the television and newspapers is influenced by the different design of the two samples.
2. Our newspaper sample has been selected with the help of a narrow range of keywords. This could have influenced the extent to which references to citizens' deliberative participation in the public sphere have been found. Our television sample therefore is more likely to show general patterns of reporting.
3. These references represent citizens as commenting on social groups and issues at home and abroad, show them reacting emotionally to an issue, and represent them making vague appeals to institutions of power (such as the government and the corporate world), as well as to fellow citizens, about a social or political issue.
4. Unlike in television news, the *New York Times* and *The Times* represented the military attacks on Afghanistan as a subject of active political debate. Newspapers were more likely to refer to citizens making a clear appeal to governments, corporate world or fellow citizens, than they were to refer to other levels of citizenship engagement. However, our samples of television news and print news were not based on the same time period. Moreover, the selection of the newspaper sample, compiled with the help of a narrow selection of key words, could have influenced the extent to which specific levels of citizenship appeared. Therefore the findings of our analysis of television news, which was not compiled with the help of key words, seem more reliable.

8   Getting engaged?

In this final chapter, we review the main thrust of our findings, and consider the consequences that arise from them. We end with some positive suggestions based on what we have learnt thus far. But first, we shall take a brief step back and take stock of the larger cultural and economic forces at work in the way we understand citizenship.

The rise of consumerism

We are addressed as consumers hundreds of times a day. Advertising has become ubiquitous, and now permeates our cultural environment. Our media system is saturated with commercials, from newspapers and magazines to an ever-growing presence in broadcast media. So, for example, governments in both Britain and the USA have allowed our dominant information and entertainment source – television – to be increasingly defined by the rules of commerce and less by the goals of public service. Our cultural industries meanwhile – from sports arenas to concert halls – are plastered with corporate come-ons. The rise of retailers like IKEA is both a symptom and a product of consumerism, catering, as it does, for our increasing need for ingeniously designed storage systems, as we buy ever more things.

Advertising clutters the landscape, from billboards and posters to shop fronts and the sides of buses and even the clothes we wear. It has turned the Internet from primarily a public information service into a consumerist tool, while the postal service – and even the phone system – is now increasingly about the delivery of publicity rather than letters. With every year that passes, another commercial-free space succumbs to this relentless commercial logic (Klein, 2002). If we trace our history up until this point, we can see that as voting has declined, consumerism has burgeoned – a rise that seems inexorable. If governments are prepared to draw a few boundaries – around products like cigarettes or alcohol, and even, for more courageous governments, against advertising on children's television – they show little sign of stemming this tide, let alone reversing it. Can we imagine, for example, regulation to *decrease* the overall volume of TV advertising?

The great irony of all this is that very little advertising is actually helpful to consumers. Advertising, after all, makes us 'better' consumers only in the sense that we buy more things. It does not provide us with balanced information – or, in many cases, with much information at all – and has allowed such a clutter of product proliferation that it is difficult to make rational decisions about quality and price. Indeed, attempts to provide useful product information – such as clear labelling of the nutritional content of food – tend to come from the public realm, from civic groups or governments, rather than from commerce.

Nor does it make us content. As Sut Jhally argues, studies show that once we have reached a certain level of material comfort, what really makes us happy are social values – rewarding work and leisure time, love, good health, friendship, strong family bonds – rather than material possessions. While economists have charted increasing levels of material wealth, surveys suggest that we are no happier with our lot that we were fifty years ago. Advertisers know this, which is why they rarely try to persuade us about the intrinsic value of the soft drink, the mobile phone, the shampoo, or even the bank account, and work so hard to associate the dead world of things with *social* values (Jhally, 1998). A commercial that tells us why and how a product is useful or worth buying now looks quaint or old-fashioned. In this 'diamonds are forever' world, advertisers try to link what they are selling – however preposterously – with freedom and fulfilment.

Just after the Second World War, retail analyst Victor Liebow suggested that:

> Our enormously productive economy ... demands that we make cosumption our way of life, that we convert the buying and selling of good into rituals, that we seek our spiritual satisfaction, our ego satisfaction in commodities ... We need things consumed, burned up, worn out, replaced, and discarded at an ever increasing rate.
>
> (cited in Durning, 1991: 153)

If this seemed a dark, Orwellian vision then, it now looks prophetic and even unremarkable. It also indicates the extent to which the drum-beat of advertising is *not* ideologically innocent. Advertising tells us that happiness is found *exclusively* in the purchase of commodities, and that the solution to every problem is to buy something. Hole in the ozone layer? Buy some factor 20 sun-cream. Obesity? Buy these diet aids or 'low fat' treats. Worried about crime? Buy these security devices – or even a house in a safer neighbourhood. It is fully in keeping with the logic of this cultural environment that the ultimate solution for social ills offered by most political parties is economic growth.

For citizens to compete against this deluge of consumerism is an uphill battle. Take, for example, two vital issues facing citizens in the twenty-first century: climate change and the terms of trade in a globalised world. Scientists or environmentalists concerned about global warming have to compete against a flood of commercial messages that urge us to consume without worrying about the consequences. Campaigns against low wages in the Third World or sweatshop labour are pitted against ad campaigns that provide soothing messages inspiring trust in brand names. In short, a cultural environment dominated by advertising is not a level playing field for citizens to debate two of the key problems of our age.

But more than this, we have allowed so much creative talent and effort to be pushed into commerce that consumerism seems so much more satisfying – so much more fun – than citizenship. As Barbara Ehrenreich puts it:

> Everything enticing and appealing is located in the (thoroughly private) consumer spectacle. In contrast, the public sector looms as a realm devoid of erotic promise.
>
> (Ehrenreich, 1990: 47)

It is partly for this reason that the news media are so important to citizenship. Outside the education system, the news is *the* place in our culture where we would expect to be addressed as citizens rather than consumers, to learn about problems with the environment and the consequences of different approaches to globalisation. Even if the news media are often partly driven by the need to sell willing audiences to advertisers, we still have a culture of journalism that values its mission to inform. The news is the place, after all, where we watch history being made. So what part do we, as citizens, play in the news? Are we seen as part of history making, or as peripheral to it?

News and citizenship

There is, in both the USA and Britain, an abundance of references to citizens and their opinions in the news media. Of the 5,658 television news items we looked at, we found 4,398 references to citizens or public opinion. While these references tend to be clustered within certain news items, during an average week, between 30% and 40% of stories make *some* kind of reference to public opinion.

As we showed in Chapter 2, our data also confirm that journalists take seriously their responsibility to speak about – or on behalf of – public opinion. The great majority of references to citizens and publics on television news –

83% – come from reporters themselves, rather than from experts (10%) or politicians (4%). And we found that the voices of ordinary citizens – vox pops – are often included in news stories to locate issues in the public sphere: four in ten references to citizens or public opinion come in the form of vox pops.

Despite the talk of the 'dumbing down' of news, citizens' voices are generally invoked in relation to civic concerns – issues like health, war, security and transport – rather than entertainment and celebrity stories. With the exception of consumerism and shopping, most of the main topics shown to be of public concern were matters of political debate.

It is also fair to point out that while citizens have only a limited access to news programmes, there is widespread awareness among news professionals of the need to engage with citizens, as well as the increasing use of citizen responses in certain genres. So, for example, news radio – already used to phone-in formats – now incorporates listener texts and emails into its broadcasts. These contributions can be substantive. In the following example from BBC Radio 5 Live, Peter Allen, host of the late afternoon news programme, read out a dissenting comment from a listener. The listener was reacting to what he felt was a degree of media hype on the day that the statue of Saddam Hussein was pulled down in Baghdad's Paradise Square following its capture by US troops.

> Quick couple of emails . . . another cynic, Richard, suggests in a city of six million, what looks like a couple of hundred young men shouting to me doesn't seem . . . 'don't exaggerate and push the Blair propaganda', that from Richard. So some people not overwhelmed by what we've seen, I would say that the scenes in that centre were undoubtedly very televisual, but from what we've heard there are a lot of people in exactly that mood, in the mood to celebrate the arrival of the American troops, it's not just a few hundred we see pictured.
>
> (Peter Allen, Radio 5 Live, 9th April 2003)

While the listener's views are over-ridden, they are, none the less, acknowledged and given airtime.

However, when we look at *how* citizens are portrayed, the picture painted by this study is less encouraging. While the news makes frequent references to citizens and public opinion, it does so with very little reference to any identifiable source of evidence. Most conspicuous by its absence is the opinion poll. Although opinion polls are the most obvious source of evidence available to journalists – and most research on the representation of the public has focused on the media use of polls – only 3% of references to citizens or publics on television news in the USA or Britain make *any* reference to polling data.

If polls are the only *systematic* form of evidence available to journalists about what citizens think or feel, protests or demonstrations are, perhaps, the most conspicuous forms of citizen activism. Protests, however, receive even less coverage than polls – in our study only about 2% of references to public opinion involved these kinds of citizen activity.

In short, as we pointed put in Chapter 2, 95% of the claims about citizens or public opinion contain no supporting evidence. Even if we take a very liberal – and sociologically questionable – view about what constitutes supporting information and include vox pops as 'evidence', we still found that well over half of all references to citizens and publics are simply unsupported claims or inferences made, in most cases, by journalists.

This means that, unless all journalists are assiduous students of polling data, the impressions created about public opinion may be misleading. This matters, because in a system when political policies and decisions are made all the time but the electorate consulted only once every few years (and even then, only in the vaguest terms), to *appear* to have public support (or little public opposition) is a key political commodity. It also matters because most evidence suggests that journalists have little real understanding of their audiences and their views, but rely on *their own assumptions and biases* when they talk about public opinion (e.g. King and Schudson, 1995; Sumpter, 2000).

Indeed, while we found that references to public opinion tend to avoid overtly political or ideological statements (an interesting finding in itself, as we shall suggest momentarily), those that did are likely to portray public opinion as right-leaning or conservative. In both Britain and the USA, our study suggests, 84% of ideologically inflected references to public opinion portray citizens as being on the right, rather than as mixed, centrist or on the left. In Chapter 3 we argued that this may indicate that journalists are often influenced by powerful stereotypes about what ordinary people think – such as 'middle England' or 'middle America' – rather than polling evidence. So, for example, despite evidence of popular support for a range of progressive policies in both countries, there is no progressive, left-leaning version of 'middle England' or 'middle America'.

While the failure to use supporting evidence may be questionable journalistic practice, more worrying, in our view, is that citizens are typically depicted by the news media as passive observers of the world, rather than active citizens with views and opinions. While they are seen to have fears, impressions and desires, they don't, apparently, have much to say about *what should be done* about healthcare, education, the environment, crime, terrorism, economic policy, taxes and public spending, war, peace, or any other subject in the public sphere.

This is partly reflected in the fact that, as we detailed in Chapter 3, our study suggests that 90% of references in the USA and 95% of references in Britain cannot be categorised anywhere on a political or ideological grid. This is not because people are speaking about a different kind of politics, but because what they are saying appears to *stop short* of any definable political opinion. So, for example, we may hear that a citizen is worried about crime or frustrated with public services, but it is generally left to politicians or experts to say what should be done to improve matters. This is the case even where a wealth of polling data exists that suggests often quite specifically, what people would like to see done.

This is manifested more clearly when we look at the level of citizen engagement evoked by references to pubic opinion. Across the board, only 4% of references to citizens and publics involve people making even vague proposals about what should be done in the world. Most of these (three-quarters) are proposals directed at government – such as the wish to see more public money spent on education. Some are proposals directed at fellow citizens (such as 'we should all pull together at this difficult time') and one in eight are proposals aimed at the business and corporate world.

This last finding should, perhaps, give us pause for thought. When we think of the volume of public relations and advertising produced by the business world telling *us* what to do, the fact that only 0.5% of references to public opinion on the news involves us telling business what to do, suggests a very one-sided conversation indeed.

Overall, we found that news paints a picture in which citizens have experiences and feelings rather than opinions. At its most political, public opinion will tend to be reactive, involving responses to politicians (such as approval ratings or 'horse-race' polls), but more commonly it has no political thrust at all. So, for example, after the terrorist attacks on September 11th, we heard how people's fear of flying had consequences for the airline industry and for the economy – fears that were, in turn, linked to government policy:

> The airlines need to win back consumer confidence. Since the attacks, flights have dropped by one-fifth; passenger loads by as much as two-thirds. The ripple effect through the economy has been devastating. But if the president leaves responsibility for oversight of security with the FAA, as he might, critics say he will do little to ease passenger anxieties.
>
> (CBS News, 27th September 2001)

But the citizen, in this account, is a childlike, fearful creature whose confidence the airline industry needs 'to win back', not an active participant with views on the range of issues raised. The *active* agencies here are industry and government – not the citizen. Instead of hearing about citizens suggesting a change in the way the government handles security policies, for example, we hear about confident or anxious consumers, who react to a situation defined by others.

There might well be many citizens who have coherent opinions about what should be done to resolve over-fishing and help failing hospitals, but they do not appear to fit into current journalistic conceptions of what news is. The result is a skewed view of the political capabilities of citizens, one that ultimately justifies an elitist understanding of citizenship. The father of elitist democratic theory, Joseph Schumpeter, suggested that:

> . . . democracy does not mean and cannot mean that the people actually rule in any obvious sense of the terms 'people' and 'rule'. Democracy means only that the people have the opportunity of accepting or refusing the men who are to rule them . . . Now one aspect of this may be expressed by saying that democracy is the rule of the politician.
>
> (Schumpeter, 1976: 284–5)

Walter Lippmann was a proponent of this model and outlined, in books such as *Public Opinion* (1922), how mass media could help bring about a democratic society of this sort. He argued that democracy was in crisis and could only be saved by a battalion of specialists and bureaucrats, including well-trained journalists, who were acting from 'inside' (cf. Splichal, 2001: 11–12) and could render comprehensible the complex and messy world of public affairs.

Elitist liberal theories, in the version offered by Lippmann, Schumpeter and others, suggest that citizens are poor judges of their own interests, and that important decisions are therefore better left to the experts – those, like scientists, who have specialised knowledge or those, like journalists, who have insider experience.

Despite the fact that Lippmann and others of his persuasion have been criticised for the anti-democratic tendencies in their thought, elitist liberal theories are still going strong in contemporary political scholarship. Michael Schudson, in his book *The Good Citizen* (1998), thus argues that the role of citizens in democratic society should be limited to a self-interested 'monitorial' role: 'Walter Lippmann was right: If democracy requires omnicompetence and omniscience from its citizens, it is a lost cause. There must be some distribution across people and across issues of the cognitive demands of self-government' (Schudson, 1998: 310).

Schudson's ideal citizen engages in self-interested 'environmental surveillance' for sheer survival. She looks for information on such issues as traffic jams, the availability of blueberries, right-wing militias, and earthquake preparedness, but does not necessarily need, nor take an interest in, purely political knowledge that obviously affects anyone other than herself and her friends and family. When taken to this extreme, the citizen of elitist political approaches is a profoundly apolitical being; someone for whom political information is the means to an end, rather than an end in itself. And this is exactly the breed of citizen we see most often on television news.

This is not surprising, but rather an overall trend in media coverage.

Nina Eliasoph (1998) studied how a group of activists discussed politics in public and private settings. Although the activists were motivated by concerns about the common good and had strong political opinions, they gave little indication of this when interviewed by journalists. Instead, they acted on the basis of knowledge about what gets covered by the mass media. And what interests journalists are not stories 'showing how citizens could influence the problem, but showing dramatic, graphic effects on common people' (Eliasoph, 1998: 219). Overall, she suggests that 'civic etiquette made imaginative, open-minded, thoughtful conversation rare in public, frontstage settings' (*ibid.*: 230).

The consequences of focusing on the personal experiences of self-interested citizens, however, is what Eliasoph describes as the 'evaporation of politics in the public sphere': the idea that it is not appropriate for regular people to talk about politics in public. This reinforces the notion that 'most people are just too dumb or narrow-minded to be good citizens' (Eliasoph, 1998: 231). In sum, public expression becomes a mere backdrop against which government leaders and experts make their decisions. The world of politics is left to the politicians and the experts, who compete to sell us positive images of themselves. When citizens are seen stating clear preferences, it is usually to either grant or refuse consent for a political party or agenda: a form of citizenship undoubtedly, but one that is both weak and commodified. In the world created by news, public opinion is little more than brand loyalty (Calhoun, 1992; Salmon and Glasser, 1995: 446).

It is in this sense that we can say that we, the public, are represented in the news more as consumers rather than citizens. Consumers are seemingly apolitical and disengaged from community decision making. They respond to the possibilities on display rather than setting the agenda. They do not make history, they react to it or simply experience it. Their power is limited to the ability to choose one product rather than another – or else, more subversively perhaps, to not buy anything at all. There is nothing *wrong* with being a consumer – if we have the means, consumerism offers both temptations and pleasures. But as a way of being, it falls far short of the ideal of citizenship that underpins democratic society.

Journalism and the constraints on citizen participation

It is, perhaps, not all that startling to find that the role of the citizen in the newsworld is a limited one. In terms of traditional news values, the 'ordinary citizen' is, almost by definition, generally excluded from news about public affairs. As we have pointed out, most citizens have no authority, celebrity or expertise, and thus have no obvious *place* in a news story, which is mainly reserved for elite sources and opinions. Yet our political system rests, in theory, on what citizens think about the world – that 'democratic politics involves public deliberation focused on the common good' (Cohen, 1997: 69). And the news *is* replete with references to public opinion, whether it is a political commentator speculating in conversation with a news anchor, or 'a person on the street' responding to a journalist's questions.

The problem is that while these references provide a constant backdrop, they remain remorselessly apolitical. Why is this? The answer is not necessarily lack of will – many journalists are as concerned as anyone about the decline in electoral participation, not least because so much 'hard' news journalism depends upon an interest in politics and public affairs. Moreover, the findings presented in this book are by no means common knowledge – most reporters or news editors do not have the time to do the kind of analysis we have done here. The three explanations we would offer have more to do with customs and practices that, while they make sense in their own terms, work against promoting active citizenship.

There is no doubt, first of all, that the ideology of consumerism has transformed our ways of thinking about individuals and their identity. We speak less of viewers, readers and listeners and more of customers and consumers; less about audiences and more about markets (e.g. Underwood, 1993; McManus, 1994). This is, perhaps, not surprising, since any commercial news service is bound by market-driven imperatives, not least the need to 'capture' audiences so that that they can be packaged and sold to advertisers. But even public service broadcasters like the BBC, to justify themselves politically, are forced to think competitively and become mired in the conceptual horizons of consumerism and the market.

Indeed, the world of politics, so central to the news, is now so imbued with the techniques of the public relations industry that, at least on a strategic level, they are almost indistinguishable (Franklin, 2004). But this is more than a question of 'spin': the language of neo-liberalism – in which consumers are sovereign and markets supreme – dominates political debate. In Britain, this means that public services are seen less as providing for the needs of communities, and more as serving the needs of individual customers. In the USA, as we saw in the previous chapter, this reached its apotheosis after September 11th 2001, when consumption became elevated to a patriotic duty. It would be surprising, in this context, if a consumerist ideology did not spill over into the newsworld.

The second explanation is very different, and involves the notions of balance and impartiality. The active citizen, with ideas about public policy, can be a difficult creature to deal with on a news service committed to giving equal weight to all sides. This is particularly true when public opinion favours clear policy preferences. If a policy is the subject of debate between political parties, showing a majority of citizens clearly taking one side or another makes it difficult for broadcasters to appear even-handed. This may account for why issue-based polls which express clear policy preferences are so abundant but so little reported.

There is an irony here: the commitment to impartiality is one of the tenets of public service journalism that is hugely popular. Most people *want* a fair and impartial news service (Brookes, Lewis and Wahl-Jorgensen, 2004). And while the concepts of balance and impartiality are difficult to define, let alone enact, they can clearly have positive consequences in the creation of an informed public. We would not want to argue that this commitment be compromised. But it may be time to rethink what it means in a way that allows the active public an important role.

But perhaps the most profound obstacle to showing active citizens on television news is the traditional top-down structure of political reporting. Studies of news have found, again and again, that politics on the news is usually about what politicians do, and not necessarily what people want them to do (e.g. Tuchman, 1978; Gitlin, 1980; Glasgow Media Group, 1980; Paletz and Entman, 1981; Kellner, 1990; Brody, 1991; Parry, 1992; Zaller, 1992; Naureckas and Jackson, 1996; Croteau and Hoynes, 1997; and Croteau, 1998). So, for example, in the British 2001 election, the issue on which public opinion was most often cited was Europe – even though the same polls showed that most people did *not* regard this as a key issue (Brookes, Lewis and Wahl-Jorgensen, 2004). This was because one of the main parties chose to make it a key election issue. In short, citizens do not set the agenda, politicians do.

This example of public opinion on Europe tells us a great deal about the way public opinion is generally invoked. Public opinion on Europe was cited *not* because most people felt strongly about it, but because it was relevant to an agenda set by political elites. Similarly, we have seen, in numerous examples throughout this book, how public opinion is generally used *in response to* or to *illustrate* a story rather than to provoke or drive a story. Instead of beginning with public opinion or the action of citizens, and use this to address the politicians, the news media begin with the politician's agenda and *then* invoke the actions, thoughts or feelings of citizens in response to this agenda.

This happens, we have suggested, not because of any desire to limit the role of citizens, but because this is, by custom and practice, the way news reporting is traditionally structured. In this context, we turn to a final and important question: in brief, is it possible to imagine news in which citizens not only play a more active role but are seen to do so? While this might involve some radical departures from time-honoured journalistic conventions that perpetuate top-down news coverage, it might also be a prerequisite for engaging a population increasingly disenchanted with democratic politics.

Enter the citizen (from stage right and stage left)

Our study suggests that there are a number of ways in which the news media might show us more active instances of citizenship and public expression simply by shifting emphasis. We should stress that we are not blaming the news media for the general pattern of decline in voting and participation in electoral politics. This would, in any event, be very difficult to establish, and we certainly don't have the kind of evidence to make such a claim. As we suggested in Chapter 1, such a decline is likely to be the product of a number of political factors, such as the Democrats and New Labour's shift to the right (alienating some of their traditional base); and a first-past-the-post electoral system that limits choice to the major parties. Some readers may find the results of our study suggestive, but that is as far as we can go.

What we would argue, however, is that the way ordinary people are represented in the news media does little to inspire active forms of citizenship, while providing many ways for us to think of ourselves as hapless consumers of big government and big business. It is fair to say that, in its current form, news is part of the problem rather than part of the solution. There is nothing inevitable about this, and we end with our own suggestions about making the newsworld a more vibrant, democratic place. As Barbara Ehrenreich puts it: ' "Necessity" is not enough: we may have to find a way to glamorise the possibility of an activist public sector, and to glamorise the possibility of public activism' (Ehrenreich, 1990: 47).

We saw some effort to do this in some of the British coverage of the 2005 general election campaign, when both the BBC and ITV made conspicuous attempts to include public voices – addressing policy issues – in their campaign coverage. But in the day-to-day life of the newsworld, we would suggest a number of areas in which these kinds of efforts might be extended.

Shifting the focus to more active forms of citizenship representation

One of our most striking findings is that the great majority of references to citizens or public opinion – over 95% – are not based on any identifiable sources of evidence. This is, by any measure of journalistic practice, difficult to defend. Thus, while reporters often refer to or invoke public opinion, they make remarkably little use of polling data. Similarly, examples of citizen activism – not only demonstrations, but any form of civic campaign – usually have to pass a high threshold to be regarded as newsworthy.

Our findings also suggest that when journalists *do* refer to evidence, we are more likely to hear about more active, engaged forms of citizenship. Indeed, more than half the references to polls or demonstrations involve more active forms of citizenship – such as making proposals or giving responses to governments – while less than 20% of vox pops or journalistic inferences do so. As a consequence, if reporters did nothing more than pay more attention to identifiable evidence about public opinion – whether polls or protests – it is likely that we would see more examples of active citizenship on the news.

So, for example, in the British coverage of public services, we heard vox pops and impressionistic accounts conveying a general sense of content or dissatisfaction about railways, the health service, and so forth. However, had reporters studied and reported on the polling data available on these topics, we might have heard more than mere complaint. What was clearly available but conspicuously absent from most reports was information about *what the public would like to see done* about public services.

Making better use of polls

Our findings (along with other studies) suggest that when polls *are* covered, they tend to be used to inform a general narrative about politicians – who's up and who's down – rather than to show what people actually think about an issue. Even when the press report their own polls at length, it has more to do with speculation about its party political consequences than any considered analysis of what the polling data really tell about people's political views.

Polls are undoubtedly blunt instruments, and their highly scripted form means that they tend to construct public opinion even as they are representing it. But since they are the *only* form of systematic evidence available to journalists, it is hard to see how the news media can speak about – let alone on behalf of – public opinion without them.

Indeed, while polls are often a weak form of democratic expression, most of the alternatives are less democratic still. So, for example, if journalists use the views expressed in popular newspapers or other news media as a guide to public opinion – as many consciously or unconsciously do – they are allowing a few elite voices to represent the many. And any considered analysis of the polling data would quickly dispel those mythical figures, 'middle America' and 'middle England', forcing us to appreciate that the range of popular views embrace ideas on the left as well as the right.

In short, we would urge journalists to use polls as a guide to *what citizens want those in power to do*, not merely as a guide to who might win an election. More radically, as Jay Rosen has argued (1999), it would be refreshing – and perhaps invigorating – to see political coverage start from the bottom up rather than the top down. Thus we might begin with what people want, and ask the politicians to respond to those demands, rather than the other way around.

Vox pops: the voice of the citizen, not the consumer

The vox pop is the extra in the unfolding drama of news. The citizen is there to provide mood, background, emotional reaction or light commentary, but will often be incidental to the central narrative. It is difficult for the citizen, cast in this role, to say very much of significance.

And yet vox pops make good television: they not only provide a kind of democratic 'reality check', but *they bring the world of politics and public affairs into daily life*. They convey, perhaps more than any other news convention, that the world of politics and public policy *matters*, and that ordinary people have a stake in it. As a consequence – and because this is the main place that citizenship is defined in news (on television news, vox pops outnumber polls by more than ten to one, and protesters by twenty to one) – they are worth taking seriously.

Since vox pops do not have to be representative (although we should be aware that regardless of intent, they carry a *burden* of representation) there is no reason that news broadcasters should not encourage their vox pop inter-viewees to express political opinions. And rather than have these simply as a backdrop to the political stage, anchors and reporters can pick up on well-made points in interviews and two-ways, thereby making citizenship part of politics and public life.

Making connections

Finally, it is worth re-examining the journalists' role in giving voice to or reflecting public concerns. Again, this is something that could be taken more seriously. This means avoiding, first of all, speculation about public opinion without any supporting evidence. But as well as this, the journalist, more than anyone else in public life, has a key role to play in making connections between the actions of politicians, business leaders and other powerful figures, and the person watching, reading or listening. Too often, viewers see the media world of politics as a parallel universe – the world of 'them' rather than 'us' (Lewis, 1991).

While some journalists do this very well already, too much news assumes an interest in and knowledge of the issues it covers. Only rarely do reporters step back and put a story into a larger context (Lewis, Cushion and Thomas, forthcoming), explaining why it is significant and, above all, why we should care about it. Recent evidence suggests that when viewers understand the broader significance of a story, their interest in it increases dramatically (Philo, 2002). Equally, the skilful use of narrative can engage viewers in ways that the 'inverted pyramid' structure of news does not (Lewis, 1991).

These points will inevitably come up against the argument that there is little time available, for reporters either to prepare, or, on television news, to tell a story. Yet making connections between, say, the latest political row and the person watching it is less a question of time than of approach. Moreover, so much news is repetitive, and so little of it is of vital importance to most people, that there is plenty of scope even in a half-hour bulletin to tell stories and explain their significance. After all, what is the value of news in a democracy if not to make such connections?

References

Albaek, E., Christiansen, P.M. and Togeby, L. (2003) Experts in the mass media: researchers as sources in Danish daily newspapers, 1961–2001, *Journalism and Mass Communication Quarterly*, 80(4): 937–48.

Altheide, David L. (2004) Consuming terrorism, *Symbolic Interaction*, 27(3): 289–308.

Anderson, B. (1991) *Imagined Communities: Reflections on the Origin and Spread of Nationalism*. London: Verso.

Asher, H. (1998) *Polling and the Public*. Washington: Congressional Quarterly Press.

Baines, P.R. and Worcester, R.M. (2003) When the British 'Tommy' went to war, public opinion followed. Paper presented to the World Association of Public Opinion Research, Prague, 17–19th September 2003.

Barnett, S. (2001) Distorting democracy: public opinion, polls and the press, in S. Splichal (ed.), *Public Opinion & Democracy: Vox Populi – Vox Dei?* Creskill, NJ: Hampton Press.

Barnett, S. and Gaber, I. (2001) *Westminster Tales: The Twenty-First Century Crisis in Political Journalism*. London and New York: Continuum.

Barnhurst, K.G. and Mutz, D. (1997) American journalism and the decline in event-centered reporting, *Journal of Communication*, 47: 27–53.

Beaud, P. and Kaufmann, L. (2001) Policing opinions: elites, science and popular opinion, in S. Splichal (ed.), *Public Opinion & Democracy: Vox Populi – Vox Dei?* Creskill, NJ: Hampton Press.

Benhabib, S. (1994) Deliberative rationality and models of constitutional legitimacy, *Constellations*, 1: 26–31.

Berger, C. (2001) Making it worse than it is: quantitative depictions of threatening trends in the news, *Journal of Communication*, 51: 665–77.

Berkowitz, D. (1987) TV news sources and news channels: a study in agenda-building, *Journalism Quarterly*, 64: 508–13.

Billig, M. (1995) *Banal Nationalism*. London: Sage.

Blumler, J. (1999) Political communication systems all change: a response to Kees Brants, *European Journal of Communication*, 14: 241–9.

Blumler, J. (2001) The third age of political communication, *Journal of Public Affairs*, 1: 201–9.

Blumler, J. and Gurevitch, M. (1995) *The Crisis of Public Communication*. London: Routledge.

Bohman, J. (2000) The division of labor in democratic discourse: media, experts, and deliberative democracy, in S. Chambers and A. Costain (eds) *Deliberation, Democracy and the Media*. New York and Oxford: Rowman & Littlefield.

Boorstin, D.J. (1961) *The Image: A Guide to Pseudo-events in America*. New York: Vintage.

Bourdieu, P. (1979) Public opinion does not exist, in A. Mattelart and S. Siegelaub (eds) *Communication and Class Struggle*. New York: International General.

Brady, H.E. and Orren, G.R. (1992) Polling pitfalls: sources of error in public opin-ion surveys, in T.E. Mann and G.R. Orren, *Media Polls in American Politics*, Washington DC: Brookings Institution.

Brants, K. (1998) Who's afraid of infotainment? *European Journal of Communication*, 13: 315–35.

Brennen, B. (1995) Cultural discourse of journalists: the material conditions of newsroom labor, in H. Hardt and B. Brennen (eds) *Newsworkers: Towards a History of the Rank and File*. Minneapolis, MN: University of Minnesota Press.

Brody, R. (1991) *Assessing Presidential Character: The Media, Elite Opinion and Public Support*, Stanford, CA: Stanford University Press.

Brookes, R. (2002) *Representing Sport*. London: Arnold.

Brookes, R., Lewis, J. and Wahl-Jorgensen, K. (2004) The representation of public opinion in the 2001 election campaign, *Media, Culture and Society*, 26(2): 63–80.

Bryce, J. (1895) *The American Commonwealth*. New York: Macmillan.

Buckingham, D. (2000) *The Making of Citizens: Young People, News and Politics*. London and New York: Routledge.

Calabrese, A. (2001) Justifying civic competence in the information society, in S. Splichal (ed.) *Public Opinion & Democracy: Vox Populi – Vox Dei?* Creskill, NJ: Hampton Press.

Calhoun, C. (1992) Introduction: Habermas and the public sphere, in C. Calhoun (ed.) *Habermas and the Public Sphere*. Cambridge, MA: MIT Press.

Capella, J. and Jamieson, K.H. (1997) *Spiral of Cynicism: The Press and the Public Good*. New York: Oxford University Press.

Christison, K. (2001) *Perceptions of Palestine: Their Influence on U.S. Middle East Policy*. Berkeley, CA: University of California Press.

Coalition Information Centers (2001) The global war on terrorism: the first 100 days, Washington, USA, London, UK, Islamabad, Pakistan, retrieved 04.11.2004, from *www.whitehouse.gov/news/releases/2001/12/100dayreport.html–81.5KB*

Cohen, J. (1997) Deliberation and democratic legitimacy, in J. Bohman and W. Rehg (eds) *Deliberative Democracy: Essays on Reason and Politics*. Cambridge, MA: MIT Press.

Comrie, M. (1999) Television news and broadcast deregulation in New Zealand, *Journal of Communication*, 49(2): 42–53.

Cottle, S. (2000) Rethinking news access, *Journalism Studies*, 1(3): 427–48.

Croteau, D. (1998) Examining the liberal media claim. Unpublished manuscript, Virginia Commonwealth University, Dept of Sociology and Anthropology.

Croteau, D. and Hoynes, W. (1994) *By Invitation Only: How the Media Limit Political Debate*. London: Common Courage Press.

Croteau, D. and Hoynes, W. (1997) *Media/Society: Industries, Images and Audiences*. Thousand Oaks: Pine Forge Press.

Cushion, S. (2004) More than a fashion statement, *Planet: The Welsh Internationalist*, 168: 77–80.

Dahlgren, P. (1995) *Television and the Public Sphere*. London: Sage.

Deacon, D., Golding, P. and Billig, M. (2001) Press and broadcasting: real issues and real coverage, *Parliamentary Affairs*, 54: 666–678.

Delli Carpini, M. and Keeter, S. (1996) *What Americans Know About Politics and Why It Matters*. New Haven: Yale University Press.

Durning, A. (1991) Asking how much is enough, in L. Brown *et al.* (eds) *State of the World, 1991*. New York: Norton.

Ehrenreich, B. (1990) Laden with lard, *Zeta*, July/August.

Eliasoph, N. (1998) *Avoiding Politics: How Americans Produce Apathy in Everyday Life*. Cambridge and New York: Cambridge University Press.

Epstein, E. (1973) *News from Nowhere: Television and the News*. New York: Random House.

Ericson, R.V., Baranek, P.M. and Chan, J.B.L. (1989) *Negotiating Control: A Study of News Sources*. Milton Keynes: Open University Press.

Ettema, J. and Glasser, T. (1998) *Custodians of Conscience: Investigative Journalism and Public Virtue*. New York: Columbia University Press.

Fairclough, N. (1995) *Media Discourse*. London: Edward Arnold.

Flyvbjerg, B. (1998) *Rationality and Power: Democracy in Practice*. Chicago: University of Chicago Press.

Foner, Eric (1998) *The Story of American Freedom*, New York: W.W. Norton.

Fowler, R. (1991) *Language in the News: Discourse and Ideology in the Press*. London and New York: Routledge.

Franklin, B. (1997) *Newszak and News Media*. London: Arnold.

Franklin, B. (2004) *Packaging Politics: Political Communications in Britain's Media Democracy* (2nd edn). London: Hodder Arnold.

Galtung, J. and Ruge, K. (1999) The structure of foreign news, in H. Tumber (ed.) *News: A Reader*. Oxford: Oxford University Press.

Gamson, W.A. (1992) *Talking Politics*. Cambridge: Cambridge University Press.

Gans, H.J. (1980) *Deciding What's News*. London: Constable.

Gans, H.J. (2003) *Democracy and the News*. Oxford and New York: Oxford University Press.

Gerbner, G. (2002) *Against the Mainstream*. New York: Peter Lang.

Gieber, W. (1964) News is what newspapermen make it, in L.A. Dexter and D.M. White (eds) *People, Society and Mass Communication*. Toronto: Collier-Macmillan.

Gitlin, T. (1980) *The Whole World is Watching*. Berkeley: University of California Press.

Glasgow Media Group (1980) *More Bad News*. London: Routledge & Kegan Paul.

Glasser, T.L. (1991) Communication and the cultivation of citizenship. *Communication*, 12: 235–48.

Glasser, T.L. (ed.) (1999) *The Idea of Public Journalism*. New York: Guilford Press.

Golding, P. and Elliott, P. (1999) Making the news (excerpt), in H. Tumber (ed.) *News: A Reader*. Oxford: Oxford University Press.

Grabe, M.E., Zhou, S. and Barnett, B. (1999) Sourcing and reporting in news magazine programs: *60 Minutes* versus *Hard Copy, Journalism and Mass Communication Quarterly*, 76(2): 293–311.

Gramsci, A. (1971) *Selections from Prison Notebooks*. London: Lawrence & Wishart.

Haahr, J.H. and Holm, H.-H. (2003) *Meget Større End Du Tror: Avislæserne og det Internationale*. Århus, Denmark: Forlaget Ajour.

Habermas, J. (1989) *The Structural Transformation of the Public Sphere: An Inquiry into a Category of Bourgeois Society*. Cambridge: MIT Press.

Hall, S., Critcher, C., Jefferson, T., Clarke, J. and Roberts, B. (1978) *Policing the Crisis*. London: Macmillan.

Halloran, J., Elliot, P. and Murdock, G. (1970) *Demonstrations and Communications*. Harmondsworth: Viking Penguin.

Harcup, T. and O'Neill, D. (2001) What is news? Galtung and Ruge revisited, *Journalism Studies*, 2(2): 261–80.

Hargreaves, I. and Ferguson, G. (2000) *Who's Misunderstanding Whom? Bridging the Gulf of Understanding Between the Public, the Media and Science*. Swindon: Economic and Social Research Council.

Hargreaves, I. and Thomas, J. (2002) *New News, Old News*. London: Independent Television Commission.

Harrigan, J. (1993) *Empty Dreams, Empty Pockets: Class and Bias in American Politics*. New York: Macmillan.

Hauser, G.A. (1999) *Vernacular Voices: The Rhetoric of Publics and Public Spheres*. Columbia, SC: University of South Carolina Press.

Henn, M. and Weinstein, M. (2002) Do you remember the first time? First-time voters in the 2001 general election. Paper presented at the Political Studies Association conference, Aberdeen, 5–7 April.

Herbst, S. (1993) The meaning of public opinion, *Media, Culture and Society*, 15: 437–54.

Herbst, S. (1998) *Reading Public Opinion*. Chicago: University of Chicago Press.

Hodgson, J. (2002) Bell accuses ITN of dumbing down, *Guardian*, 19 February.

Jackson, J. (1996) Sex, polls and campaign strategy, in J. Naureckas and J. Jackson (eds) *The FAIR Reader: An Extra Review of Press and Politics*. Boulder, CO: Westview.

Jhally, S. (1998) *Advertising and the End of the World*. Northampton, MA: Media Education Foundation.

Kalberg, S. (1993) Cultural foundations of modern citizenship, in Bryan S. Turner (ed.) *Citizenship and Social Theory*. London: Sage.

Karpf, A. (1988) *Doctoring the Media: The Reporting of Health and Medicine*. Routledge: London.

Kellner, D. (1990) *Television and the Crisis of Democracy*. Boulder, CO: Westview.

King, E. and Schudson, M. (1995) The press and the illusion of public opinion, in T.L. Glasser and C. Salmon (eds) *Public Opinion and the Communication of Consent*. New York: Guilford Press.

Kitzinger, J. (2000) Media templates: patterns of association and the (re)construction of meaning over time, *Media, Culture and Society*, 22(1): 61–84.

Klein, N. (2002) *No Logo: No Space, No Choice, No Jobs*. New York: Picador.

Krosnick, J. (1989) Question wording and reports of survey results: The case of Louis Harris and Associates and Aetna Life and Casualty, *Public Opinion Quarterly*, 53 (Spring): 107–13.

Kull, S. (2003) *Misperceptions, the Media and the Iraq War*, unpublished manuscript, Program on International Policy Attitudes, University of Maryland.

Kull, S. (2004) *The Separate Realities of Bush and Kerry Supporters*, unpublished manuscript, Program on International Policy Attitudes, University of Maryland.

Ladd, E.C. and Benson, J. (1992) The growth of news polls in American politics, in T.E. Mann and G.R. Orren (eds) *Media Polls in American Politics*. Washington DC: Brookings Institution.

Larson, S. (2003) Misunderstanding margin of error, *The Harvard Journal of Press/Politics*, 8(1): 66–80.

Lewis, J. (1991) *The Ideological Octopus: An Exploration of Television and its Audience*. New York: Routledge.

Lewis, J. (2001) *Constructing Public Opinion*. New York: Columbia University Press.

Lewis, J. (2004) Television, public opinion and the war in Iraq: the case of Britain, *International Journal of Public Opinion Research*, 16(3): 295–310.

Lewis, J., Cushion, S. and Thomas, J. (2004) *24/7: an analysis of rolling news in the UK*, unpublished manuscript, Cardiff School of Journalism, Media and Cultural Studies.

Lewis, J., Cushion, S. and Thomas, J. (2005) Immediacy, convenience or engagement? An analysis of news channels in the UK, *Journalism Studies*.

Lewis, J. and Speers, T. (2003) Misleading media reporting? The MMR story, *Nature Reviews Immunology*, 3(11): 913–18.

Lippmann, W. (1922) *Public Opinion*. New York: Macmillan.

Lippmann, W. (1925) *The Phantom Public*. New York: Harcourt, Brace.

Livingstone, S. and Lunt, P. (1994) *Talk on Television: Audience Participation and Public Debate*. New York: Routledge.

Loviglio, J. (2002) Vox pop: network radio and the voice of the people, in M. Hilmes and J. Loviglio (eds) *Radio Reader: Essays in the Cultural History of Radio*. New York and London: Routledge.

Manning, P. (2001) *News and News Sources: A Critical Introduction*. London: Sage.

Marvin, C. and Ingle, D.W. (1999) *Blood Sacrifice and the Nation: Totem Rituals and the American Flag*. Cambridge: Cambridge University Press.

Maxwell, R. (2002) Honor among patriots? *Television and New Media*, 3(2): 239–48.

McChesney, R. (2000) *Rich Media, Poor Democracy*. New York: New Press.

McChesney, R. (2002) September 11 and the structural limitations of US journalism, in B. Zelziger and S. Allan (eds) *Journalism After September 11*. London: Routledge.

McManus, J. (1994) *Market-Driven Journalism – Let the Citizen Beware?* Newbury Park, CA: Sage.

McNair, B. (2000a) *Journalism and Democracy: An Evaluation of the Political Public Sphere*. London: Routledge.

McNair, B. (2000b) Journalism and democracy: a millennial audit, *Journalism Studies*, 1(2): 197–211.

McNair, B., Hibberd, M. and Schlesinger, P. (2003) *Mediated Access: Broadcasting and Democratic Participation in the Age of Mediated Politics*. Luton: University of Luton Press.

Merritt, D. (1995) *Public Journalism and Public Life: Why Telling the News is Not Enough*. Hillsdale, NJ: Lawrence Erlbaum Associates.

Miller, M. and Riechert, B.P. (2001) The spiral of opportunity and frame resonance: mapping the issue cycle in news and public discourse, in S. Reese, O. Gandy and A. Grant (eds) *Framing Public Life: Perspectives on Media and Our Understanding of the Social World*. Hillsdale, NJ: Lawrence Erlbaum Associates.

MORI (2001) How Britain voted in 2001, *British Public Opinion*, XXIV (3/4): 3.

Naureckas, J. (1991) Gulf War Coverage: The Worst Censorship Was At Home, *Extra: Special Gulf War Issue*.

Naureckas, J. and Jackson, J. (eds) (1996) *The FAIR Reader: An Extra Review of Press and Politics*. Boulder, CO: Westview Press.

Neuman, W.R., Just, M.R. and Crigler, A.N. (1992) *Common Knowledge*. Chicago: University of Chicago Press.

Nie, N., Junn, J. and Stehlik-Barry, K. (1996) *Education and Democratic Citizenship in America*. Chicago: University of Chicago Press.

Norris, P. (2000) *A Virtuous Circle: Political Communications in Post-Industrial Democracies*. New York: Cambridge University Press.

Ouellette, L. (1999) TV viewing as good citizenship? Political rationality, enlightened democracy and PBS, *Cultural Studies*, 13(1): 62–90.

Page, B. (1996) *Who Deliberates? Mass Media in Modern Democracy*. Chicago: University of Chicago Press.

Page, B. and Shapiro, R. (1992) *The Rational Public*. Chicago: University of Chicago Press.

Paletz, D. and Entman, R. (1981) *Media Power Politics*. New York: Free Press.

Parry, R. (1992) *Fooling America*. New York: Morrow.

Peters, J.D. (1995) Historical tensions in the concept of public opinion, in T.L. Glasser and C.T. Salmon (eds) *Public Opinion and the Communication of Consent*. New York: Guilford Press.

Philo, G. (2002) Television news and audience understanding of war, conflict and disaster, *Journalism Studies*, 3: 173–86.

Putnam, R.D. (2000) *Bowling Alone: The Collapse and Revival of American Community*. New York: Touchstone.

Rawls, J. (1997). The idea of public reason, in J. Bohmann and W. Rehg (eds) *Deliberative Democracy: Essays on Reason and Politics*. Cambridge, MA: MIT Press.

Richards, B. (2004) The emotional deficit in political communication, *Political Communication*, 21: 339–52.

Riddell, P. (1999) Creche course, *Guardian*, 20 September.

Rosen, J. (1999) *What are Journalists For?* New Haven: Yale University Press.

Salmon, C.T. and Glasser, T.L. (1995) The politics of polling and the limits of consent, in Salmon and Glasser (eds) *Public Opinion and the Communication of Consent*. New York: Guilford Press, 437–458.

Salwen, M. (1995) News of Hurricane Andrew: the agenda of sources and the sources' agendas, *Journalism & Mass Communication Quarterly*, 72(4): 826–40.

Schlesinger, P. (1999) Putting reality together (excerpt), in H. Tumber (ed.) *News: A Reader*. Oxford: Oxford University Press.

Schudson, M. (1998) *The Good Citizen: A History of American Civic Life*. New York: Free Press.

Schumpeter, J. (1976) *Capitalism, Socialism and Democracy*. London: Allen & Unwin.

Schurr Kirsten (2001) *Racism in Reporting, Jingoism as Foreign Policy*, Retrieved 6th January, 2004, from http://www.mediamonitors.net/kristenschurr1.html

Seldner, J. (1994) Voice of the privileged, *Nieman Reports*, 48(1): 89.

Sigal, L.V. (1973) *Reporters and Officials: The Organization and Politics of Newsmaking*. Lexington, MA: D.C. Heath.

Sigal, L. (1986) Sources make the news, in R.K. Manoff and M. Schudson (eds) *Reading the News*. New York: Pantheon.

Smith, A. and Porter, D. (2004) *Sport and National Identity in the Post-War World*. London: Routledge.

Speers, T. (2004) The MMR vaccine: a public relations crisis or misplaced scientific debate? Unpublished doctoral dissertation, Cardiff School of Journalism, Media and Cultural Studies, Cardiff University.

Splichal, S. (2001) Introduction: public opinion and democracy today, *Public Opinion and Democracy: Vox Populi – Vox Dei?* Creskill, NJ: Hampton Press.

Steele, J. (1995) Experts and the operational bias of television news: the case of the Persian Gulf War, *Journalism & Mass Communication Quarterly*, 72(4): 799–812.

Sumpter, R.S. (2000) Daily newspaper editors' audience construction routines: a case study, *Critical Studies in Media Communication*, 17(3): 334–46.

Sussman, G. (2005) *Global Electioneering: Campaign Consulting, Communications, and Corporate Financing*. Lanham, MD: Rowman & Littlefield.

Thompson, E.P. (1968) *The Making of the English Working Classes*. London: Penguin Books.

Tuchman, G. (1972) Objectivity as strategic ritual: an examination of newsmen's notions of objectivity, *American Journal of Sociology*, 77: 660–79.

Tuchman, G. (1978) *Making News*. New York: Free Press.

Tzanelli, R. (2003) 'Casting' the Neohellenic 'other': tourism, the culture industry, and contemporary orientalism in 'Captain Corelli's Mandolin', *Journal of Consumer Culture*, 3(2): 217–44.

Underwood, D. (1993) *When MBAs Rule the Newsroom*. New York: Columbia University Press.

van Dijk, T. (1998) Opinions and ideologies in the press, in A. Bell and P. Garrett (eds) *Approaches to Media Discourse*. Oxford: Blackwell.

Wahl-Jorgensen, K. (2002a) Coping with the meaninglessness of politics: citizenspeak in the 2001 British general elections, *Javnost/The Public*, 9(3): 65–82.

Wahl-Jorgensen, K. (2002b) The construction of the public in letters to the editor: deliberative democracy and the idiom of insanity, *Journalism*, 3(2): 183–204.

Welch, R.L. (2002) Polls, polls, and more polls: an evaluation of how public opinion polls are reported in newspapers, *Press/Politics*, 7(1): 102–14.

Zaller, J.R. (1992) *The Nature and Origins of Mass Opinion*. Cambridge: Cambridge University Press.

Index